D1630898

# The Legend of Pryderi

## FIONA COLLINS

SERIES ORIGINATOR: FIONA COLLINS

The History Press

*I Marian.*

*Bydded i'r adar gyd-ganu*
*yn gerddgar i ti*

First published 2013

The History Press
The Mill, Brimscombe Port
Stroud, Gloucestershire, GL5 2QG
www.thehistorypress.co.uk

© Fiona Collins, 2013

British Library Cataloguing in Publication Data.
A catalogue record for this book is available from the British Library.

ISBN 978 0 7524 9005 2

Typesetting and origination by The History Press
Printed in Great Britain
Manufacturing managed by Jellyfish Solutions Ltd

# Ancient Legends Retold: An Introduction to the Series

This book represents a new and exciting collaboration between publishers and storytellers. It is part of a series in which each book contains an ancient legend, reworked for the page by a storyteller who has lived with and told the story for a long time.

Storytelling is the art of sharing spoken versions of traditional tales. Today's story-tellers are the carriers of a rich oral culture, which is flourishing across Britain in storytelling clubs, theatres, cafés, bars and meeting places, both indoors and out. These storytellers, members of the storytelling revival, draw on books of traditional tales for much of their repertoire.

The partnership between The History Press and professional storytellers is introducing a new and important dimension to the storytelling revival. Some of the best contemporary storytellers are creating definitive versions of the tales they love for this series. In this way, stories first found on the page, but shaped 'on the wind' of a storyteller's breath, are once more appearing in written form, imbued with new life and energy.

My thanks go first to Nicola Guy, a commissioning editor at The History Press, who has championed the series, and secondly to my friends and fellow storytellers, who have dared to be part of something new.

*Fiona Collins, Series Originator, 2013*

# Acknowledgements

My thanks first to my partner Ed Fisher: for his beautiful illustrations to the story, for living through the whole process of writing and telling Pryderi's story with me, and for his love and support.

Next I would like to thank these friends and fellow storytellers, who have advised and supported me during my journey: Ronnie Aaronson, Katy Cawkwell, Wendy Dacre, Amy Douglas, Fiona Eadie and June Peters.

My thanks to Aberystwyth Storytelling Festival, the Spirit Horse Foundation and

Stroud Storytelling Circle for opportunities to tell Pryderi's story, and to the musician Jem Hammond who worked on it with me in performance.

I first published a written version of the story of Rhiannon's meeting with Pwyll as a short story, 'Rhiannon: Lady of the Horse People', which appeared in the anthology *A Stone for Remembrance*, published by Y Lolfa. Some material from that version is reworked here, with the publisher's permission.

I am grateful to my friends and fellow Welsh learners, the tutor Maria Haines and the poet Peter Jones for help with the section on pronunciation, to the team at *Network News* for generously offering me the chance to begin writing Pryderi, and most of all to my editor at The History Press, Nicola Guy, whose enthusiasm and commitment brought this series of Ancient Legends Retold into being.

Finally, my thanks to my friend Robin Aaronson, who chose to dedicate this book to the memory of his mother Marian, in sup-port of the Forest of Dreams, a noble cause to which he, I and our friends have long been committed. The Forest of Dreams is a charity set up to care for a beautiful valley in mid-Wales and to preserve it as a place of sanctuary for humans and the wild.

www.forestofdreams.org.uk

# Introduction

Storytelling is a vital part of the way we humans make sense of the world and, as such, it has existed since the earliest times. The stories known as The Four Branches of the Mabinogion, from which 'The Legend of Pryderi' is drawn, come from an ancient and authentic source. The oldest surviving versions of these tales are found in two fourteenth-century Welsh language manuscripts: the White Book of Rhydderch, written about 1350, and the Red Book of Hergest, dated between 1382 and 1410. The first is in the care of the National Library of Wales in Aberystwyth, the second in the Bodleian Library in Oxford, and both can be consulted online.

The Four Branches first came to the attention of a modern audience when Lady Charlotte Guest published them, together with eight other tales from the manuscripts, in a scholarly, bilingual work, which she brought out in seven volumes between 1838 and 1849. New versions continue to be published today, in Welsh, English and other languages.

It is clear, from their structure and form, that the medieval manuscripts are written forms of oral tales. As such, the stories may be much older than the versions in the Red and White Books.

Storytellers living in Wales, and of Welsh descent everywhere, have reason to be proud of these stories, though nothing can be known of their earliest tellers. Some scholars have suggested that they were composed for, or even by, the Welsh princess Gwenllian at her court in Deheubarth in south-west Wales, during the early twelfth century. They are unique in the oral corpus of the islands of Britain, and still intrigue us today.

Only one character appears in all Four Branches. He is Pryderi, the hero of this book. My interest in Pryderi comes from long exploration of the material of the Four Branches and from my work as a storyteller, retelling the tales in my own words, first in English, and more recently in Welsh, to people of all ages. I have always searched for ways to make this material speak clearly to modern listeners. I have also explored the connections of the Four Branches with the landscape of Wales. I have done this by walking the land, returning again and again to places associated with the stories, and also by taking part, during the late 1990s, in some of the courses on 'Storytelling and the Mythological Landscape', which are still run annually by my fellow storytellers Hugh Lupton and Eric Maddern at Ty Newydd Writers' Centre in north-west Wales.

In 2008, I had the good fortune to be invited to write for *Network News*, a monthly publication which the editors call a 'guide to inspiring events in North Wales'. They had been thinking, for some time, of including a story in the magazine, to run as a serial over twelve months. They kindly agreed to let me choose my own subject matter, and so, thanks to them, I was able to explore Pryderi's story in depth over an extended period, tracing it through all Four Branches. This was the genesis of my performance work with the story and, eventually, this book.

Following Pryderi from Branch to Branch has enabled me to make many important connections which are not obvious in the Branches themselves, for though Pryderi is a principal character in both the First and the Third Branches, the parts he plays in the other two are much smaller. I found that focusing on his role shed new light on events and characters throughout the stories. For example, the first time that the Birds of Rhiannon are mentioned is in the Second Branch, when they are heard singing at Harlech by the seven warriors who are the sole survivors of a war in Ireland: when I realised that one of the seven was Pryderi, Rhiannon's son, the song of her birds took on a whole new resonance, which I decided to foreground in my version.

I have tried to draw out the themes which speak to me in Pryderi's story, which I tell as a hero's journey. In my version we accompany him on the life-journey which we all must make: the journey from birth to death. Pryderi is a child lost and found; he gains temporal power and then true love; he proves himself as a warrior, yet experiences the suffering caused by war; he wins a companion and mentor; he faces the confusions of magic and enchantment. In each major episode I believe he has a lesson to learn and an aspect of true humanity to earn.

Entwined with Pryderi's story we find strong women living out their life-journeys too: Rhiannon, his mother, whose own story is so encompassing that it threatened at times to eclipse Pryderi's in the writing; and Cigfa, his wife and heart's companion, who rules while he is at war and holds faith for him while he is under enchantment. This story can speak to us all, as any good story does, in our quest to call up and consider our true nature.

I hope you will be as inspired by the 'Legend of Pryderi' as I am. If you are moved by this version, find your own way to share it, in whatever form you choose. If it does not speak to you, please do not give up on this extraordinary story, but go back to a translation of the Four Branches and make your own meaning from what you find there. The old stories have much to offer to those who care to listen.

# The Names in the Story

## Some general advice on Welsh pronunciation

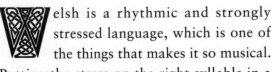elsh is a rhythmic and strongly stressed language, which is one of the things that makes it so musical. Putting the stress on the right syllable in a word is a huge step towards pronouncing it correctly. The stress almost always falls on

the last syllable but one. The stressed sylla-ble is indicated in the guide below by *bold italic*. If a syllable is added to a word, for instance to make it plural, the stress moves accordingly (e.g. *can*tref, but can*tref*i).

Welsh is written almost phonetically, but some sounds are difficult to make with an 'English mouth'.

DD is a soft 'th' sound, created by letting your tongue protrude slightly between your teeth and blowing over it (like the sound of 'th' in 'this' or 'that').

FF is the sound 'f' in English (e.g. in 'if'). F in Welsh makes the sound 'v' (e.g. in 'of').

G is always pronounced as in English 'go', never as in 'giraffe'.

LL is a different 'th' sound, this time cre-ated by putting your tongue behind your top teeth, as if to start the word 'Liverpool', and blowing gently out of the sides of your mouth without making any sound in your throat.

R should be rolled a little if possible.

RH is not really heard in English: the nearest sound would be in 'perhaps' when it is pronounced 'p'raps', with something of a trill to the R.

Y has two sounds: in a word like 'Pryderi' it is unstressed and sounds almost like 'uh': (think of the first sound in 'under'). However, in Pryderi's father's name, Pwyll, the 'y' sounds like the 'i' in 'with'. Aberystwyth contains both pronunciations of 'y' in one word, though you won't find it in this book. The first 'y' is 'uh' (and carries the stress, as it's in the last syllable but one). The second 'y' makes the 'i' sound of 'with'. So: 'Aber-*ust*-with'.

# Important personal names in the story and how to pronounce them

Bran, giant King of Gwynedd: braan (long 'a' as in 'arm', not as in English word 'bran').

Cigfa, Pryderi's wife: *keeg*-va ('va' to rhyme with 'ha', not 'far').

Efnisien, half-brother to Bran, Branwen, and Manawydan: ev-*niss*-yan.

Gilfaethwy, brother to Gwydion the sorcerer: gil-*vay*-th'-wee ('gil' as in 'give' not as in 'giraffe').

Gwawl, Rhiannon's thwarted suitor from the Otherworld: goo-*owl* ('goo' as in 'good').

Gwri, Pryderi's child-name: *goo*-ri ('goo' as in 'good', 'ri' as in 'Richard').

Gwydion, sorcerer from North Wales, brother to Gilfaethwy: goo-*wid*-yon ('goo' as in 'good', 'wid' as in 'widow').

Heilyn, one of the seven survivors of the war in Ireland: *hay*-lin.

Llwyd, Rhiannon's enemy from the Otherworld: *loo*-wid (see note on 'll').

Manawydan, Bran's brother, Pryderi's friend, and later Rhiannon's second husband: man-ah-*wid*-an ('man' with long 'a', as in English word 'man', 'ah' as in 'arm', not as in English word 'bran').

Pryderi, hero of this story: pruh-*der*-ee (see notes on 'y' and on rolling 'r').

Pwyll, Pryderi's father: poo-*wi*-l (see notes on 'y' and 'll').

Rhiannon, Pryderi's mother: rhi-*yan*-on (see note on 'rh', 'i' as in 'with').

Teyrnon, Pryderi's foster-father: *tayr*-nun ('ay' as in 'navy', see note above on rolling 'r').

IMPORTANT PLACE NAMES IN THE STORY AND HOW TO PRONOUNCE THEM

Dyfed: *Dove*-ed.

Gorsedd Arberth: *gorse*-eth *ar*-birth (see note on 'dd').

Gwales: goo-*wa*-les ('goo' hardly pronounced at all, 'wa' with long 'a' as in first syllable of 'artificial', 'les' like the shortened form of 'Leslie').

Gwent-is-Coed: goo-*went*-iss-koyd ('goo' as in 'good', 'iss' to rhyme with 'hiss', not 'his', 'oy' as in 'boy').

Gwynedd: goo-*win*-eth ('goo' as in 'good', see note on 'dd').

Lloegr: *loy*-grr (see note on 'll', 'oy' as in 'boy', 'grr' as in the noise a tiger makes, see note on 'r').

Maentwrog: mine-*tour*-og ('tour' as in French pronunciation of 'Tour de France', 'og' as in 'hog').

## Other important Welsh words used in the story

Cantrefi, the plural of cantref, literally meaning 'one hundred town', the medieval word for a division of land: kan-*trev*-ee.

Hiraeth, Welsh for a melancholic nostalgic longing, an emotion for which there is no exact word in English: *here*-ay-th ('ay' as in the personal pronoun 'I', 'th' as at the beginning of 'thing').

Pryder, meaning 'trouble', 'worry', or care', the key word in Rhiannon's exclamation when she was reunited with her son, from which Pwyll, his father, decreed Pryderi's name: *pruh*-dare ('uh' as in 'under').

Tynged, meaning a fate, duty or obligation: *tongue*-ed.

# The Legend of Pryderi

The story begins here: a pitched roof, earthen walls, a wooden door with its upper half ajar in the gathering dusk, lantern light slanting out through the slats of the door, a smell of hay and harness and horses ...

Here is a mare: she is a warm chestnut in colour, with a sheen upon her sweating flanks. She is shaggy-maned, taut-bellied, her head low and legs trembling with the strain, as she pushes out her foal into the world.

Picture the foal she gives birth to there: a fine young creature, wobbling to his feet, turning his head this way and that, eager to see his brave new world. He has a white blaze on his forehead and white socks on his front legs. His coat is dark at first sight, but it lightens as the mare cleans him, until he shines as she does, and she is content.

Watching over them is a horseman with strong, capable hands and a quiet, gentle voice. He soothes the mare as she gives birth, supporting the foal as it slips into the world, encouraging the mother to lick her foal clean, watching the foal painstakingly fold the long stilts of its legs until it can lie down to rest, the mother nuzzling it in beside her.

But after the birth he does not go back to the warmth of his hearth, to sit by the fire and sip warm honey ale and recount the night's story to his wife. For this is Teyrnon, Lord of Gwent-is-Coed in south-east Wales, and for the last two years he has tended his prize mare, bringing the stallion to her in spring, watching through the summer as her belly swells, waiting patiently through the winter. For the last two years, both times on May Eve, he has settled the new foal safe beside its mother, before returning to his hall to celebrate the addition to his herd. But each year, by the time the morning of May Day has dawned, the foal has been gone, the mare standing dolefully, head down, sniffing at the straw where it had lain.

Teyrnon has decided that enough is enough.

So on this May Eve, as the story begins, he settles the mare and the foal, then crouches in the shadows of the stall, a naked sword across his knees: watching as the animals slip into sleep ... listening for any sound of menace from outside the safety of the stable.

He listens. And waits. Nothing happens. Until ...

In the very darkest part of the night, the stable door blew open.

But there was no wind.

The straw rustled.

But nothing moved.

The mare stirred.

But there was no one there.

Until menace came: and when it did, it was soundless.

It was as though time had frozen. The night seemed to be holding its breath. Everything was still and silent. Teyrnon, his every muscle taut and tense, was like a stone, unmoving in the dark, though the hairs rose on the back of his neck. Then a shadow fell across the open door. Moonlight gleamed on a cruel, curved, sharp shape.

In through the stable door reached something dark and menacing. Teyrnon could just make out a huge scaled limb, its claw, crooked and taloned, stretching out to close silently around the foal. The only warning came from the mare, which started and stamped, snorting in fear. But now he was ready, all his senses alert, his stillness turning to action, so that he burst from his dark corner in an explosion of energy. Before the claw could close around the helpless animal he raised his sword in a two-handed grip and struck, severing the sinewy limb with a single slash, so that the claw clashed and clattered, spurting hot blood, onto the floor. As the bleeding stump was snatched away, he heard the howling of a wounded creature outside. He raced outside to finish the beast. But it had gone, limping away to some distant lair, leaving only a trail of blood and the echo of its pain behind it.

But something else was left behind, too. Teyrnon almost missed it, for it was no more than a darker patch in dark shadows. But it made some small, weak, helpless noise, and that caught his attention, even as he stood there panting, leaning on his sword. He looked around, still on his guard, though already some instinct told him that the source of the sound was harmless. He waited, and waited, but heard nothing else. Then, just as he relaxed his attention, it came again.

'Not an animal,' he thought, trying to identify the source of the sound, 'but it is something living.'

His bloodstained sword held high, he moved quietly towards the shadow of the stable wall, alert and ready – or so he believed – for anything. But what he saw, when he peered down into the darkness, was the very last thing he had expected to see: a bundle wrapped in a pale woollen blanket, apparently shapeless, apparently still, with no limbs visible. Now he doubted his senses once again: this looked too inert to be the source of any signs of life. But then, from within the indistinct form, the sound came again – and at last he recognised it for what it was: the laboured breathing of a human baby about to cry, a baby that had been clutched and carried away by the nameless creature, just as had almost happened to the foal. A baby that had been dropped by the creature as it fled, mortally wounded. With a wordless exclamation, Teyrnon sheathed his sword, reached down, and picked up the bundle.

So enters the hero of this tale.

Teyrnon carried the baby into his stronghold. His wife, who had lived for many years with the ache of unwished-for childlessness, felt her heart melt when he put the swaddled bundle into her arms.

'Let us keep him and raise him as our own,' she whispered to her husband. 'Who knows where he came from? There is no way to find out. I can tell my women I have been secretly pregnant, and that the child is mine. I would love him so!'

'He is strong and sturdy, and wrapped in good wool,' said Teyrnon. 'This blanket is fine work. Surely he is the son of some noble family. He needs to be taken care of. We will do it. We will care for him. He will want for nothing.'

'Yes,' smiled the childless woman, childless no longer, pushing back the edge of the blanket to caress the fair down on the baby's head. 'We will name him Gwri Golden Hair:

for his bright fuzz of hair, for the bright future we shall give him!'

So the child who had been lost was found, and given a name to see him through his childhood. The foster parents who took him in were kind and gentle and good to him. Gwri thrived, and Gwri grew.

In fact, he grew so swiftly and so well that by the time he was one year old, he was as big and strong and capable as a three-year-old. By the time he was two years old, he was as big and strong and capable as a six-year-old, and by the time he was three years old, he was in the stables all the time, pestering the grooms and stable boys to let him groom, let him feed, let him ride ... let him help them with the horses.

His foster mother watched the boy fondly. She spoke to her husband, 'What happened to the foal you saved on the night that you found our boy?'

'It is running free in the fields with the herd,' replied Teyrnon. 'It's a fine colt. I am well pleased with it.'

'Would it not be a good idea to have the horse gentled and readied for riding, and give it to the boy? For they were both born on the one night, and the saving of one led to the finding of the other.'

'It is a good idea,' agreed Teyrnon. 'Why don't you give it to him?'

They called Gwri to them, and he came running in from the stables. His foster mother said, 'Son, you do well with the horses, and it is time you had one of your own. The colt with the white blaze is three years old, and soon he should be backed. If he takes after his mother he will be a spirited steed. Would you like to have him, and start to teach him, with our help?'

Gwri's eyes were as bright as his hair, and he nodded breathlessly, wordlessly, while his foster parents smiled down at him.

So the horse was given to the boy, and they were well matched, and made a fine pair. The horse and his boy went everywhere together from that time on.

Time passed, as time does, until seven years had gone by since the night when Gwri had been found. His foster mother doted on him, and loved him dearly, and seemed to have blotted out any memory that he was not her own birth child. But Teyrnon wondered, now and again, when he looked at his foster son – especially when the lad was galloping over the meadows on his little stallion – what his origin might have been, and whether, somewhere, his family was pining for him, his father grieving for the loss of his heir.

Then a traveller came through, trading leather goods from the kingdom of Dyfed in the South West, a place well known to horsemen like Teyrnon for the quality of the tack and harness which was to be had. As was the custom, the traveller asked for, and received, the hospitality of the house: a bed for the night and food for his belly. And, as was the custom, he shared in exchange the news and stories he carried with him. So Teyrnon and his wife, sitting at their own hearth, heard for the first time all that had been happening in Dyfed.

'Our king, Pwyll, is a good man, and a good king. But he is not happy. He married a beautiful woman, a queen from the Otherworld, the place of magic. Some people said he should have married a woman of our own kind, a woman of Dyfed. But I think they were very happy, for a time. Some people said that when she came riding out of her world into ours, she put a spell on him to enchant him and win his heart. But I think that he truly fell in love with her, and she with him. They were married, and it was a joyful time. The whispers against her were silenced then, for a time.

'They waited a long time for a child to come, and some people said he should put her aside, and choose another queen, but he would not. When the queen at last became pregnant, everyone rejoiced, and those who had spoken against her were silenced again.

Their child was born on May Eve, and word was brought to Pwyll that he had an heir. But our king never saw his son. When he went to see the baby on that bright May morning, there was no sign of him. The child had disappeared.

'Some people said that the midwives had seen terrible things: that they told how, in the middle of the night, the queen tore her child to pieces and devoured him, and they could not prevent her, for she had the strength of a wild thing, and overcame them all, though they were six and she but one. Some said she should have been killed for that, that she was a murderer. All the city was alive with talk of it. The king would not kill his wife, for he loved her still, but he had to punish her. The people demanded it. I do not know who devised her punishment, but it is a cruel one. The queen has been set down from her throne, and instead must sit by the mounting block at the gate of the city. She must tell everyone who comes there the terrible story of the loss of the child – her terrible story – and offer to carry them on her back wherever they would go, as if she were a packhorse.

'But the queen had three birds which were always about her, and they sang so sweetly that the sound would soften the hardest heart. Those birds have not been heard since her punishment began. It is a great loss, almost as great as the loss of the king's smile, the queen's happiness. I do not think that anyone blessed with such birds could be as evil as they say …'

'Nor do I,' said Teyrnon thoughtfully.

'No more do I,' said Gwri, whose cheeks were flushed, whose fists were clenched. 'What is her name, this unfortunate lady?' he asked.

'Rhiannon. Rhiannon of the Birds.'

Gwri said no more, but Teyrnon noticed how his lips moved silently, making no sound, but forming that name over and over again.

Teyrnon was calculating dates and making connections. He considered his foster son, and thought how very much the lad resembled the King of Dyfed as he had been when a youth, for King Pwyll, as was the custom for the sons of noble families, had been in foster-age nearby as a boy. Teyrnon recalled seeing him many times at the hunt, and remembered how, as a young man, Pwyll had loved horses as much as Gwri now did.

Once traveller and boy were both asleep, Teyrnon and his wife sat by the embers of the fire, talking in low, urgent voices.

'Did you note when it happened? Do you know when that was?'

'Yes, the same night that you found our boy and brought him in from the stable. Do you remember the blanket, so finely made?'

'I said it showed he was of noble blood.'

There was a silence. Then Teyrnon asked, 'Could you bear to let the boy go?'

She answered with a different question. 'Could I bear to leave a mother suffering because she does not know where her child is? Our boy's future is not in our hands. He has a fate of his own. Our part in it is over.

Go to the court, my dear. Take our son with you. Take his baby blessing blanket with you too, to show the proof of our tale.'

So it was agreed that Teyrnon would ride with Gwri to the court of King Pwyll, to declare the truth about his lineage, and his destiny.

———◆———

On the day that Teyrnon arrived with his foster son at Pwyll's court, the man on his brood mare and Gwri on the little stallion that shared his birth date, Rhiannon the Queen was waiting at the mounting block by the city gate. This she had done, day in, day out, for all the long years since the disappearance of her child, continuing to endure the cruel punishment imposed on her then. As they approached, she stood up. They saw a tall woman, her head low and her shoulders hunched. Her clothes, which had clearly once been rich and fine, were ragged and dusty, and her hair hung in knots about her face.

A smear of dirt marked her cheek, as though she had rubbed a grubby hand across it, with no care for how she looked. It was clear, to anyone who had eyes to see, that she was beautiful, but that her beauty no longer held any joy for her. She waited until they had dismounted at the block, but stopped them with a gesture as they made to enter the city. She held her head as though it were a great weight on her neck, and looked at them with dull eyes. Then, in a flat voice devoid of expression, she told her story yet again, the story she had been made to tell over and over in the long years since her punishment was decreed.

'Sirs, I killed my child, I ate my child, on the night of his birth. I am required to carry on my back every visitor to the city. This is my punishment for killing my child. Where do you wish to go?'

'My lady,' replied Teyrnon, 'I could not abide to let you bear me. We are bound for the King's Court, but I do not think that either of us will let you carry us there.'

'Whoever might, I never would.' The boy spoke up firmly. His voice seemed to startle her, and she lifted her eyes to his. And who knows whether, when she looked into his eyes, some connection was felt between them, in that moment at the gate where three roads met.

And perhaps because of that connection, Rhiannon did something then, that she had never done in all the long years of her punishment: she walked alongside the travellers who had refused to let her carry them, her head held high and her back straight, looking all the time at the young boy whose eyes had met hers. She accompanied them into the King's Great Hall, and the guards were so astonished to see her, walking once more like a queen, that they stood aside and bowed to her, as though she had but then stepped down from her throne, instead of enduring long years of disgrace. So she entered once more her husband's presence.

And that is why, when Teyrnon told his tale, both king and queen were listening. As he described how, in defending his horses against some monstrous assailant, he had found a stolen baby, wrapped in fine wool, all eyes turned to the boy beside him. And hearing his own true tale told by the one he thought of as his father, though he knew he was not the man who had fathered him, the boy looked back curiously at them all, with eyes that very much resembled the eyes of the king, set above a nose that was very like the nose of the king ... the evidence was there for all to see. No one really needed to see the little blanket that Teyrnon brought out to show. Rhiannon did not even need to see the boy's face. She already knew in her heart that this was her son. When the story was done, she cried out, from her heart, *'Duw'n dist, petai hynny'n wir, fe fyddai'n fodd o gael gwared o'm pryder i.'* Which is, in the other language of this land of two tongues: 'As God is my witness, if that were true, I should be glad to be relieved of my care [*pryder*].'

'Lady,' replied Teyrnon. 'It surely is true.
Everyone here can see from the boy's face
that he is the son of the king.'

The king said, 'Indeed, it is so. He is
returned to us, and we thank you from our
hearts. To mark this moment, he shall have a
new name – and what would be better than
the one his mother, the Lady Rhiannon, gave
to him, in the first words she spoke on knowing him once more? He shall be called Pryderi
from this time on.'

So the lad was named for the care that his
mother had suffered, and which was washed
away when she was reunited with him. And at
that moment, Rhiannon's three birds, which
had been absent for so long, flew in through
a window and circled above her, singing so
sweetly that every heart was softened.

Now began the time for Pryderi, who had
been Gwri, to come to know the mother and
father he had never seen before. He had also
to bid farewell to the ones who had raised
him. When Teyrnon left for home, the boy

remained at the court of his newly discovered parents, to begin the life of a prince.

He left behind his childhood name and everything else he had grown up with, saving only the clothes he stood up in, and the horse with the white blaze that had been born on the night of his own birth, and given to him by his foster parents. This was all he brought with him into his new life.

There were thanks and honours and gifts and promises of everlasting friendship for Teyrnon and his wife, for the saving and the raising of the heir to the throne, though it is doubtful whether any or all of these could compensate for the loss of the child they had found and cared for and loved. But they knew they had done what needed to be done, and though they shed tears at losing their golden-haired boy, they always held their heads high.

And so Teyrnon returned to his own lands, and Pryderi (from now on we shall know him by the name his birth parents gave to him) began the life of a young prince, heir to the kingdom of Dyfed.

Time passed, as time does. Pryderi thrived, and he grew. In not much more time than it takes to tell, or so it seemed to his mother, he grew from a child to a youth, and from a youth to a man. For Rhiannon, the time passed all too quickly. She treasured every day with her son. She would have held time still, to savour each moment he was with her, to make up for the seven lost years. But this she could not do, in spite of the powers she undoubtedly possessed. For she was, indeed, as the traveller's tale had unwound, a woman of the Otherworld, who had chosen to leave her own people and come to live with, and love, a human man. So instead of stopping time, she beguiled it, by telling Pryderi the stories of his family. She told him her story: of her own world, and how she had left it behind for love of his father. And he listened.

'I entered this world, and your father's life, while he watched for a wonder from the top of Gorsedd Arberth, the magical hill near his court. I rode out of the West and into his heart on my great grey mare.

'This is how it was: nobody was awake to see me rise from my sleeping place while the air was still dark; the day was only a lemon-yellow smudge on the eastern horizon, the pale moon still nodding low in the sky.

'I led my mare out into the cool morning air. I mounted from a rock, and turned the horse towards the mouth of the valley, urging her away from the encampment.

'"Come now," I whispered, "My dear one, my swift one, let's see if we can break through, or if it's impossible, as the old ones would have us believe."

'You see, the leaders and wise ones of my people were long familiar with the places where worlds touched, and the windows through which one could see into the world of humans. I knew that this was powerful and secret knowledge, and that I was not permitted access to it.

'But I, by chance, had found one of these openings, behind a waterfall, when I stopped to let my mare drink one day. Through the sheen of rushing water, I could see the human world. I saw there a dark man, taut as a coiled spring. The men of the human world had always seemed to me coarse and vulgar. But he was different ... He had something of both worlds in him, and also something of his own, that I had never met before. That, of course, was Pwyll, who was to be my husband and your father.'

Pryderi nodded contentedly. He liked to hear of his own place in her story.

'I had not forgotten him: often, since that day, I had gone secretly, silently, to watch him, there, and at other windows between our worlds. Once I had found that first one, they became clear to me wherever I went. I did not know who this man was, nor his place in the world of humans. But I wanted to know. So I decided to ride out, to break through, to find and to meet and to test him, in his own world. I knew that this was forbidden, that I was breaking the laws of my people even by thinking of it. But none of that mattered.

'I cantered down the valley. The mare's pounding hooves matched my heartbeat. I was moving easily with the horse's rhythm, galloping now, on sure hooves. My own world was all around me – grey, tawny, dappled in the early light.

'Then, beyond the rocky slopes of the mountains, I saw it! In the valley, shimmering air: a doorway between the worlds, an entrance to the human world.

'The air felt thick as water. Two worlds flickered and overlaid each other in the doorway at the valley mouth. I could see my own world, pale and dew-drenched, gilded by the morning sun. I could also see the human world, vivid and colourful. I glimpsed gay pennants unfurling, glossy horses jostling, bright figures gleaming in the strong strident colours of that world.

'It was like looking into a river pool and seeing at once both the stones at the bottom and the reflection of sky and clouds. My eyes seemed to dance between the worlds.

'And suddenly I burst through! Into the human world, breaking the surface like a sleek-headed seal. Everything was sharp and definite, brightly coloured and clear-cut, the way I remembered it from that first time of seeing. I was moving in both worlds. In my own, the mare was galloping, racing forwards; yet, here, in this other world, we were moving ahead together slowly; ambling, at an easy pace.

'I crossed a grassy meadow, riding away from the river, which flowed, it seemed, through both worlds. The land sloped gently upwards in front of me, towards a small, round-topped hill.

'There I saw him, the one I had been looking for.'

Pryderi nodded. He loved to hear of his father and mother's first meeting.

'Your father was sitting on the top of that hill, a few young warriors beside him, and he was looking out over the valley: alert for anything.

'Then, out of the blue, he saw me. He leapt to his feet, staring in my direction, shading his eyes; then he turned to a young lad beside him, pointing down the hill, speaking urgently. I saw the lad bend his knee respectfully, then come running down the hill towards me.

'"So," I said to myself, holding the mare on her headlong course towards the hill, "He commands men, and they readily obey him. Who is he?"

'As my horse moved forward in one world, and the man ran down the hill in another, our paths in both were converging.

'In my own world, I was galloping, galloping. I saw the dumbstruck face of the young runner, one arm raised as if to signal me to stop, his eyes following me as I passed him. But I did not stop. I merely circled the hill, turned my horse back towards the gateway at the valley mouth, and broke through again into my own world.

'Of course, in this world, your father, at the top of the hill, saw things from a different point of view. He saw me approaching slowly, the horse ambling. And yet he saw me pass the bottom of the hill just as his runner arrived there; saw me moving away from his messenger, the gap between us widening, even though the boy was soon running with all his power, and I was only moving slowly, at an easy pace. The runner strained and strained, but could not catch up with me. At last he had to stop, gasping for breath, then he turned back, and slowly, on legs like lead, made his way to where his lord waited at the top of the hill.

'"Who is she?" your father must have asked himself, as the red-faced runner bent his knee to apologise for failing in his lord's command. Then, more loudly, so that all should hear, "No, no, you are not to blame. You did all you could. We all saw the way things went.

There is some magic at work here. We shall return now to court. But tomorrow, at this same time, let all who would follow this adventure come back with me. And this time, lad, bring your swiftest horse!"

'And, with that, your father led his people home.'

Pryderi nodded again. He liked to think of his father, brow furrowed, wondering what had happened.

'The next day, in our two worlds, we were both ready, watching. To tell the truth, I had thought of little else in the intervening hours. I think, perhaps, the same was true for your father.

'When I broke through into his world, I knew where to look this time. I saw him again, watchful at the top of the small hill, his people around him. I noted the horse tethered at the bottom of the hill. Its clean lines spoke of swiftness. But I laughed to myself.

'I whispered to my mare, "They won't catch us, will they?" Then I set her galloping towards the hill, feeling once more the over-lay of two worlds: speeding over the ground in my own world, moving at an easy pace in his.

'He must have known I was there almost before he saw me; noting my distance from the hill, the relaxed tempo of my approach, the easy task which lay before his rider ... or so he thought! Even so, he was not taking any chances. He nodded to the lad, who waited only for permission to be gone, straining like a hound on the leash.

'When the runner reached the bottom of the hill, I was not yet level with it. As he put his foot into the stirrup, I was approaching. When he settled in the saddle, I was just a pace or two in front of him. As he turned his horse to follow me, it must have seemed to the watchers at the top of the hill that there was only a pace or two between us. Yet, of course, he could not catch up with me!

'He set his horse into a trot, moving brightly, urgently, over the ground. My horse was walking, but he could not close the gap between us. He urged his horse into a canter, moving swiftly, smoothly over the ground. He could not gain on me, though my horse's speed seemed only the half of his! He put his horse into the gallop, and it sprang away – neck outstretched, ears flat, long legs eating up the ground. He could not match my horse, which moved so slowly, ambling along at an easy pace!

'At last he had to admit defeat, and turn his spent horse back towards the hill. And I rode home once more through the doorway between the worlds, laughing with the thrill of the chase.'

Pryderi nodded. This was something familar, something he too loved; the delight of being as one with the horse. He almost drifted away into a reverie of his own. But his mother's story drew him in once more.

'Your father would not give up. "We shall try again tomorrow," he declared. "And this time I shall have my own horse here, the fastest in my stable. I will not renounce this adventure. I will meet and know this lady!"

'The long day crept past, as we went about our separate lives, in our separate worlds. But, to be honest, we had no thought save for each other.

'With the morning, we both set out once more for the meeting place between the worlds.

'He left his horse tethered at the bottom of the mound, climbed to the familiar place, and looked towards the west, waiting for me to reappear; knowing, somehow, that I would not be long in coming.

'I came cantering down the valley and through the gateway, full of wonder that something so extraordinary could so quickly have become familiar.

'I saw him. He saw me. As I approached the hill he leapt up, and started to run down the slope. He vaulted into the saddle and brought his chestnut horse round to face me. He urged the horse after me. The chase was on!

'He fixed his eyes on me. He could scarcely believe what he was seeing. Though the mare's pace was no faster than an easy walk, she was moving away from him. He whispered to his mount and leant forward over its neck.

'I was looking straight ahead now, resisting the impulse to watch him over my shoulder as I pulled ahead. I knew he was following me; I was straining to hear the sound of his horse's hoof beats.

'He was struggling to keep up with me, seeing me draw further and further away. At last, in desperation, he called out, "Lady, for the sake of the one you love the best, stop, turn and wait for me!"

'Ha! He had spoken to me! I halted immediately, and turned the mare so that she was facing him. I watched him come close, and rein in his mount only a pace or two from me. I looked at his handsome, puzzled face.

'"I am willing to do so," I answered, "And it would have been better for both you and your horse if you had asked me sooner!"

'He nodded ruefully at that, and asked, "Lady, where do you come from, and where are you going?"

'I said, "I am about my own business, and I am glad to see you."

'"I welcome you," he said. "Will you tell me anything about your business?"

'"I will. My most important business was to see you."

'His face broke into a smile, and joy brightened his eyes. "That seems to me the best business you could be following! Will you tell me your name?"

'"Lord, I will," I said. "My name is Rhiannon: Rhiannon of the Birds."

'"And mine is Pwyll. I am the lord of these lands."

'And as we spoke, and smiled, and laughed together, a great love was born between us. And my birds flew down and circled us, singing so that I thought my heart would burst with the sweetness of it. And from that moment we were promised to each other.'

Pryderi smiled. He loved this story, the tale of how his parents met, because it reminded him of his link with both worlds, through his father and mother.

She told him everything she could of the Otherworld: of pale dawns and nights bright with stars; of dancing rings and hollow hills; of ceremonies and rituals; the good and the bad.

She told him of the hill where his father had waited and watched. 'It is one of the doorways between the worlds, and a place that is marked out as one where a man of noble blood may match himself against magic. Your father tested himself there, and though his horses were too slow to catch up with me, he himself was not found wanting!'

Rhiannon told Pryderi, too, of the marriage that would have been forced upon her if her beloved Pwyll, his father, had not rescued her. She told of how together they had driven away her Otherworldly suitor, a man named Gwawl, with a cruel trick.

'Your father came to my world to marry me, and we sat down to a great feast. But the man who wanted me played a cunning game, which he almost won, because your father is so soft-hearted.'

Pryderi chuckled at this. He knew the story well enough to be confident that all would turn out well. Were his father and mother not happily living together, as the proof of this? Rhiannon continued her tale.

'In the middle of the wedding feast a petitioner came in, asking your father for a boon. In the generous foolishness of his great heart, he merrily cried, "Whatever you ask for, you shall receive, on this, my most happy day!" I quailed at this, for when the fellow pushed back his hood I could see well enough that he was the man I had rejected, Gwawl by name, and I could see too how his eyes gleamed with triumph. He asked then for my hand in marriage, and my wedding feast, to be given to him instead of to Pwyll. Of course your father had had no idea who this was, and now he was stunned. But what could he do? He had given his word. He stared at me in horror, and I said to him, "Be silent as long as you like. You could not say anything more foolish than the words that have already passed your lips."

'"Is there nothing we can do?" he asked me.

'I leaned close then to whisper, for his ears only, "This thing may yet come out right, if you will trust me and do all I say. I will tell him that, though you must keep your word as regards renouncing marriage to me, this feast is not yours to give, for it was set out by my family for our guests. You must tell him that a new feast will be prepared for him, a year from tonight, and at that feast I will marry him." Pwyll stared at me, but I signalled to him to trust me, and he did.'

'What happened then?' asked Pryderi, though in truth he knew well where the story would go. Rhiannon laughed at the memory.

'A year later, Gwawl was sitting beside me at the marriage table. His eyes were gleaming once more, and he thought he had won. But then a beggar came in, all dressed in rags, humbly asking for some food from the feast, as much as would fill his little bag. So Gwawl ordered the servants to fill the bag, but they could not do so, however much they put in. Then Gwawl, a man of scant patience if ever there was one, snarled, "Will this bag never be full?"

'And your father – for it was he, all in disguise – said the words I had taught him, "Sir, the bag will only be full when a man of noble birth steps into it with both feet and declares, 'Enough has been put in here!'"

'The rest was simple, for the bag was a magic one that I had given to your father. I urged Gwawl to do what was asked, saying that it would be the only way to get rid of the fellow who was spoiling the feast. At last, with a grunt, he stepped down from the high table and put his feet into the bag. At once your father and I stretched that magic bag until it reached right over Gwawl's head, and we trussed him up in it.'

Pryderi giggled, but now Rhiannon's face was solemn.

'Pwyll stripped off his ragged disguise, and blew his horn to call in his followers. They beat Gwawl, beat him in the bag, until he sued for mercy. Pwyll made him promise to renounce all claim on my hand, and bound him never to try to take revenge for what had happened. All this he swore, so that they would let him out of the bag. A sorry sight he was, limping out of the court, supported by his kinsman Llwyd, covered in scraps and smears of food from inside the bag. They called it a game, called it Badger in the Bag, but in truth it was a deep humiliation for a man like Gwawl.

'I am not proud of what we did to Gwawl,' she said. 'Your father and I had won each other, but it cast a shadow over our wedding. There were some who were opposed to my union with the mortal world, unhappy about the shaming of Gwawl by a human … However, I am glad beyond words that I married your father, not Gwawl. We made him vow never to seek revenge, and he bound himself with his word to leave us in peace. He had to. I never saw him again. Nor thought about him, either.

'Your father and I celebrated our marriage and, after the wedding, held a feast. Then I came back with him, to this world, to his kingdom, to be queen at his side. Your father and I were happy together, truly happy. My birds sang melodiously in those days. When I found I was pregnant with you, our happiness was made even more complete – until you were born, and we lost you, all in the one night.

'That was a terrible time. The midwives blamed me for what had happened while they slept, when they should have been watching over you and me, on our first night together. And while I slept, and they did too, in the darkest part of the night, something happened. You were taken. Gone. Within a few hours of your birth, you had been stolen away. And by what?'

Pryderi opened his mouth, eager to answer, to tell her the tale he knew, of the clawed monster that had stolen him from her, only to drop him outside Teyrnon's stable when it reached for other prey. But, of course, Rhiannon too now knew this part of the story. Smiling, she put her finger to her lips, nodded her head, and continued her tale.

'The midwives did not know what had done it, only that they would be blamed for not keeping watch, for sleeping when they should have been working. So they put the blame on me.

'When I woke and reached for you, and found you were not there, I was confused, uncertain. I turned to the midwives, asking, "Where is he? Where is my baby?" The women stared back at me, stony-faced. Gone were the encouraging smiles and sympathy which had surrounded me during the birth. They were no longer on my side, helping me to bring my baby into the world. Now, all they wanted to do was cover up your disappearance and avoid any blame.

'They spoke all at once, calling in your father and the high officers of the court. Their words were shocking to me:

"We could not stop her."

"We tried to stop her."

"She was too strong for us."

"She murdered the child. She murdered your child, Lord."

"Lord, we tried to warn you."

"Why did you not listen to our words?"

"This woman is a stranger."

"She does not come from our world or follow our laws …"

"She is a danger."

'Their voices became shrill. But the next that I heard was measured, thoughtful. Your father's most trusted advisor spoke, "My Lord, you cannot let this matter rest. The courts must be brought in. There must be an official investigation. There may need to be a trial."

'Pwyll looked full of confusion and grief. He shook his head slowly, trying to clear his mind. He gazed doubtingly at me. When he finally spoke, his voice was deliberate, though dulled with grief. "Very well, let there be a trial. We must find out what has happened to the heir to the throne … to my son."

'And then he turned away, and would not meet my eyes. I was too shocked, too confused, to protest my innocence. And no one spoke up for me as I wept for my lost son. Even my birds left me, and their song was heard no more.

'Only when you came back to us at last, looking so like your father, did my joy return, my birds sing again. My son, I am glad to have you here, to be able to watch you grow. But don't grow too quickly – such a lot of time was lost, which I want to make up!'

Pryderi laughed, and hugged his mother. He loved her, and understood that she meant well when she urged him not to grow up and away from her. But inside he was eager, like so many young people, for the power and freedom of adulthood. For him there was the promise of a throne and a kingdom, and perhaps glory and a lasting memorial in song and story. He could hardly wait!

He learnt well, and quickly, the skills on which a king must call to protect his kingdom; the wisdom that is needed for the business of good government; the lie of his land; the stories of his people and his place. He spent some time at court, and some in fosterage, as was the custom then for the noble-born, learning the best ways to live from the good example of those his parents chose.

Almost as fast as it takes to tell, Pryderi was a young man, well taught in statecraft and the ways of the warrior, well versed in the stories of his people, with all the skills that were needed to become a king.

And needed they were, sooner than even Pryderi would have wished.

One morning Pwyll, his father, rode out to the hunt, tall and gay as always on his fine bay horse. However, at nightfall he was brought home pale and broken, carried on a litter. The stallion had stumbled and fallen as it careered through the wild wood, breaking its leg and rolling on its rider as it fell, so that both horse and man lost their lives in the same moment.

The people of Dyfed mourned, for he had been a good king. Rhiannon, who had loved her husband deeply, withdrew from the life of the court, and her birds ceased to sing. Pryderi's time to be king was upon him, though neither the time nor the circumstances were as he might have wished. To him was given the crown, the throne and the kingdom. He became King of Dyfed.

He was a young king, a good king, with wise counsellors around him, to help and advise him. He inherited a beautiful and fertile land, which he ruled wisely and well, so that all his people loved him: seven regions, or *cantrefi,* in all. In due course he conquered and added to them another seven, and the kingdom grew and prospered.

He made a love match with Cigfa, the beautiful daughter of one of the noble families of the land, and a great wedding feast was held.

And this could be the 'happy ever after' moment, which is so often signalled in story by a wedding or a feast. But there is more than 'happy ever after' to Pryderi's tale, which takes him on a hero's journey through a long and eventful life, filled with tragedies and triumphs, victories and defeats, bright times and dark.

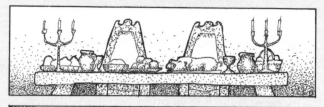

Pryderi was a good king. The kingdom of Dyfed prospered under his rule, as it had in his father's time. He proved to himself, and to his people, that he knew how to be a king. However, he was aware that he had not yet led out his troops on the battlefield, to face the test of war. A young king wants to be tried as a warrior, and not found wanting. A new king wants to know he can defend his kingdom. A true king protects his people and their land in times of both peace and war. He knew this in his heart, much as he, his beloved Cigfa, and all his subjects, delighted in the peaceful times that prevailed under his rule. He knew too that the first loyalty of a king is to his people. But the second is to his allies.

So, when a call to arms came, for Pryderi it meant that a time of testing had come, and with it a chance to measure his own worth as a warrior. With bright blasts of trumpet, a herald rode in from Gwynedd in North Wales, calling on the lords of the land to bring their forces to the aid of the giant king, Bran. The cause was to right a wrong which had been done to his sister, Branwen, by the people of Ireland.

Pryderi did not hesitate, but raised his war band and set out northwards, entrusting to Cigfa and Rhiannon the care of the kingdom until his return. His wife and mother could only do what wives and mothers have always done: watch their man go away to war, waving him off with encouraging smiles on brave faces, their hearts full of fear and their minds full of unanswerable questions: will he come back to me alive, or dead? Broken, or whole? Will he be lost to himself and to me in the horrors of war? Will he ever be the same?

But Pryderi turned his back to home and his face to the adventure, and headed northwards, untried, untested, and eager to be so. He had never met the giant king, known to all as Bran the Blessed, nor his brother Manawydan and their half-brothers, nor indeed their beautiful sister Branwen, in whose name the standards of war had been raised. However, this was of no importance. Another Welsh king had asked for help, and ties of friendship and prudence made it incumbent on him to take action.

As he journeyed, meeting others responding to Bran's call, Pryderi learnt more of the story from his new companions at arms.

'The King of Ireland came to Harlech some years ago seeking an alliance with King Bran, and the Lady Branwen's hand in marriage to seal the agreement.'

Pryderi nodded. For women of noble blood in those days and those times, marriage was more often a matter of politics than love. His own marriage to Cigfa had joined him with a woman he loved dearly, but had also brought the loyalty of her father and brothers, and more land under his rule. It was no surprise to hear of a treaty accompanied by a wedding.

'But Branwen's twisted half-brother Efnisien soured the whole thing by creeping into the stables and mutilating the horses of the Irish. This he did, they said, for spite and jealousy.'

Pryderi knew what a great insult to the Irish king this would have been.

Bran the Blessed had offered new horses and gifts aplenty in recompense. At the time, the Irish had been appeased by this gesture and by Bran's assurances that his half-brother's wicked act had been committed without either his knowledge or approval. The marriage contract was upheld and the feast renewed. When the Irish returned to their land, Branwen sailed with them as their new queen.

Memories are long, however, and insults are hard to forget. Feeling had eventually turned against the new Queen of Ireland, even though she had borne the king a son and heir. Branwen had been stripped of her crown and sent to slave in the kitchens, where she endured a multitude of humiliations.

When Pryderi heard this, he remembered his own mother's shaming, and how she had suffered for years after he had been lost, because she too was always considered an outsider. He was filled with empathy for Branwen.

But Branwen was nothing if not resourceful. In her lonely state, she befriended a starling, sharing with the bird the crusts that were all she was given to eat, gentling and taming it until it would come readily to feed from her hand. Then she tied a letter to its wing, a scrap of paper, a few words, and sent it out across the sea, to carry news of her plight to her giant brother. The starling proved as devoted to Branwen as the Birds of Rhiannon were to Pryderi's mother. Somehow it crossed the wildness of the Irish Sea, and found its way to Bran at Caer Seiont, his stronghold on the River Arfon.

The small messenger landed in the huge palm of the giant king, and when Bran read the message it carried, he was filled with fury. He raised his war band, and sent out riders to his neighbours and allies, calling for their support to attack Ireland, to rescue and avenge Branwen.

All this Pryderi learned on the long road from Dyfed to Bran's stronghold. From there he took ship to Ireland with the massed armies. Bran's son Caradog remained as steward of the land in his father's absence. Only seven warriors stayed behind with Caradog, and they governed from a place in the Vale of Edeyrnion. To this day it is still called Bryn Saith Marchog, the Hill of Seven Knights.

As the fleet of ships moved out into the sea, carrying the flower of the warriors of the land, Pryderi looked ahead from the deck of Bran's warship, staring westwards to the horizon, straining to make out the distant shape of Ireland. Then he turned round, to see his homeland as never before, from the sea. He watched the land recede in the distance. And saw something strange: a mountain pushing out into the waves! At first he could make no sense of what he saw. Then he realised that he was looking at the giant King Bran, striding out into the sea. Too huge to be contained in any structure, whether house, hall or warship, Bran was setting out to wade through the sea to Ireland. So great was his impatience to reach the foe that he would not wait for the wind. Instead, he shouted for ropes to be thrown to him, and began to haul the entire fleet behind him.

'This will strike wonder into the hearts of the enemy,' chuckled Pryderi to himself.

Indeed, when the Irish lookout saw the strange sight looming in the distance, the only words he could find to describe it to his king were, 'Lord, a mountain is crossing the sea, surrounded by a forest of tall trees! I saw two mighty lakes on the slope of that mountain, with a great ridge between them.'

The King of Ireland turned to his wise men and advisors, asking them to explain. No one could unriddle this mystery. But Branwen, in her servant's rags, was passing through the back of the hall, a pile of dirty dishes in her hands. Hearing the words of the lookout, she put down her load, and laughed out loud, for the first time in many a long day. Then she spelled out the meaning of the sight to the Irish court.

'The mountain that you see is my brother Bran coming across the ocean to rescue me. Those two lakes are his eyes, and the ridge his nose. As for the forest, it is made up of the many masts of the ships of my people, coming here to avenge the wrongs I have suffered. And you do well to be afraid!'

Her words turned the king cold with fear.

'We cannot prevail against such a foe,' he said, 'and it would be better to avoid battle if we can. We will abandon the stronghold and retreat to the heartland. Order the men to break down the bridges over the rivers behind them as we go, so that the enemy cannot follow us.'

So it was, when the war bands of Bran and his allies came ashore, that they found the Irish stronghold empty and everyone long gone. They did not tarry, but set out in pursuit, following their enemy's tracks inland,

and making good progress, until they came to the bank of the great River Liffey. There they were forced to halt. They saw the ruins of the bridge, and they saw too that the river was too wide to cross and too deep to wade, the current too swift to swim. At first it seemed as though the army would get no further.

So Bran showed them all what it means to be a true king. '*A fo ben bid bont*,' he said, meaning: 'Let the one who would be a leader be a bridge.' And with that, he lay down in the mud and stretched his huge frame across the river, bank to bank, so that all the warriors, all the warhorses, and all the weapons could cross the river on his back. When word of this deed reached the Irish, they were cowed, and sued for peace, for they knew in their hearts that they were in the wrong in this matter.

Peace indeed seemed within reach, and a happy ending too. Branwen was restored to her high place, her son once more in her arms. Remorse and forgiveness were expressed, and vows of friendship were reaffirmed between her husband the king and her brother the king.

But Branwen's half-brother Efnisien was not so easily appeased, for the mischief in his heart made him always ready to turn all that was good to evil. At the feast of celebration and reconciliation, he leapt to his feet and snatched Branwen's son from her, throwing the boy into the fire to suffer a dreadful death before her very eyes. Thus he deprived his sister of her only child, and Ireland of its heir. His senseless and evil act precipitated a bitter battle. In the bloodbath that followed, men slashed and slayed until the rivers ran red. There was no victory for either side, nor much honour in that conflict.

Of the Irish host, not one warrior was left alive, they say, and of the Welsh, only seven survived. These are the names of the seven: Manawydan, brother to the king; Taliesin the Bard; Ynawg; Glifiau, son of Taran; Gruddieu, son of Muriel; Heilyn, son of

Gwyn; and Pryderi, sickened by slaughter and longing for home.

The Irish king was killed outright. King Bran was wounded in the thigh with a poisoned spear, a harbinger of certain death. He called his seven remaining followers to him, and set *tynged* upon them: that is, a fate or obligation which he required them to fulfill.

'You must strike off my head, before the poison completes its course through my body and kills me. Take the Lady Branwen safely home and carry my severed head with you back to Gwynedd. Then I ask you to undertake a strange and wonderful journey in my name. Carry my head first to my castle at Harlech, where we made the ill-fated marriage contract which bound my sister. There you shall remain and feast for seven years.

'Then you must take the head to the island of Gwales, which lies both off the coast of Pembroke and somewhere altogether outside this world. There you may stay for eighty years in a great hall with three doors, and I promise you that my head shall be as good company to you there as it was while still on my shoulders.

'As long as you refrain from opening the door facing out towards Aber Henfelen, the Severn Sea, you shall remain there, out-side time, and the head will not decay. But if ever you open that fateful door, you will no longer be able to stay, and must take the head to London, and bury it there, on the White Hill. Only when you have completed all these tasks which I command of you, will you be free to return to your homes and loved ones once more.'

The seven accepted the destiny that Bran had laid upon them, and vowed to do all that he required of them. It would have been ignoble to do otherwise. As for the rest of the ill-fated royal family of Gwynedd, Efnisien had perished in the battle, and only Branwen and Manawydan survived. Like Pryderi,

Manawydan returned from battle whole in body, though perhaps not in spirit, after surviving so senseless a slaughter.

So Branwen and the head of her giant brother crossed the sea once more to Wales, in the care of the seven remaining warriors. They came ashore at Aber Alaw, on Ynys Mon, the Island of Anglesey. When Branwen stood at last once more in her native land, she gazed around, then turned and looked out to sea, back towards Ireland. 'So many lives lost, both here and there. And all because of me,' she whispered.

With that, she gave a great sigh and fell to the ground, her heart broken and her will to live extinguished by the horror of all the death and destruction wrought in her name. She could not be revived. The seven wept for her, and for themselves. Then they buried her on the bank of the River Alaw, where the stone marking her grave can still be seen today.

Once they had laid Branwen to rest, and mourned her loss and all the blood spilled in her name, Pryderi and his companions still faced the task that Bran had set for them as he lay mortally wounded: to undertake a magical journey in the company of his still-living severed head. As he had required of them, they set out first for Harlech. There they feasted long in Bran's great castle by the sea.

Meat of the best and wine of the full glass were prepared for them, so that they might rest and refresh themselves. They gazed at the laden table, remembering something of how things had been for them before the war. Then they sat down to eat. No sooner were they seated at the high table than three birds began to sing to them, a song of such sweetness that they had never heard its like. The birds were so far out to sea that they could scarcely be seen in the distance, yet their song was as clear as if they were perched among the rafters of the great hall.

Pryderi went to the window and looked out at the birds. 'They are my mother's birds,' he cried. 'They are the Birds of Rhiannon!' He was greatly comforted by their song. In fact, all seven weary warriors gained solace from the presence of these magical birds, whose song, it has been said, could raise the dead, or lull the living to sleep.

For seven years the companions remained in Harlech, feasting and resting and listening to the healing songs of the Birds of Rhiannon, until they were fully restored. But at the end of that time, bound as they were by the destiny laid upon them by Bran, they were constrained to set out again on their journey.

They travelled southwards until they reached the coast of Pembroke, and from there took ship to the little island of Gwales, which is also called Grassholm. There, as Bran had foretold to them, they found a fine hall above the sea. It was just as he had described: they saw that it had three doors, two of which were open, and a third which was closed, facing towards the sea.

'Bran has warned us not to open the door that is closed,' said Pryderi.

'That is the one,' indicated Manawydan, as the seven went in through the two open doors.

As they entered that hall, they stepped out of this world and out of time. When they settled down to sleep that night, they were content, and lacked nothing. And the mystery – and the blessing – of the place was this: they remembered nothing of all the sorrow that they had seen and suffered, nor did they have any awareness of the sadness and grief of this world.

Pryderi and his companions spent eighty enchanted years there, listening to the stories told by Bran's head, the tales that were old when this tale was only just beginning. They enjoyed peace and tranquility such as they had never known before. The time passed without any of them ageing a single day, nor, it seems, did time pass in the world outside that magical hall. Their stay in that magical place has come to be known as the Assembly of the Noble Head. Who knows what Pryderi learned in that time, what wisdom he gained, what tales were told?

Perhaps he might have remained there forever, and fallen quite out of the world of heroes and legend, becoming lost in the mists of myth, if one of the seven had not broken Bran's interdiction, and set time running once more …

Heilyn, son of Gwyn, spoke out suddenly one day, shaking off the delicious languor which the magic of the island had extended over them all. 'Shame on me,' he said, 'if I do not open that door and see whether what Bran said about it is true.'

'Don't do it,' said Pryderi, 'for Bran warned us not to.'

'By my beard,' retorted Heilyn, 'I will open it.'

Manawydan, a cautious and temperate man by nature, rose to reason with him, but it was too late. Before anyone else could speak or stir, Heilyn had opened the third door. What they saw through it was unremarkable: the distant coast of Cornwall and Aber Henfelen, the Severn Sea. But what they felt was profound. It was as if the opening of the door opened also the doors of perception, allowing all their memories and all their sorrows to rush in upon them again. Furthermore, as the door was opened, time began to turn once more. The Noble Head closed its eyes and lips, and spoke no more. It began to decay.

They could no longer remain. Their sojourn beyond the bounds of space and time was over. Bran had foreseen this, as he had foretold their whole long story. The time had come for them to set out on the final stage of their journey. That journey took Pryderi eastward, out of his own land and, for the first time, into Lloegr, England.

The seven companions carried the head to the great city of London, founded by the god-king Beli on the banks of the mighty River Thames, as the old tales tell. There, as Bran had bade them, they buried the head on the White Hill. It was said that as long as the head remained concealed there, it would protect the island from invasion. It is also said that in later times King Arthur ordered it dug up, claiming that he could defend the land by the strength of his arm, and had no need of enchantment to help him do so. What became of the head, the story does not say, but long years after this part of the story, the Tower of London was built on the White Hill. Bran's totem bird, the Raven, still flourishes there today.

Once the Noble Head was buried, the task of the seven was completed. Pryderi and his companions were at last freed from their obligation to Bran. Their heads full of thoughts of their loved ones, they took leave of each other and prepared to return to their homes, in order to pick up the threads of their lives once more. However, Manawydan made no move, but sighed and said, 'I am the only one who has no place to go tonight.'

Manawydan had lost his whole family and his right to the crown in the confusion that followed the death of Bran and the wholesale loss of the warriors of Wales. He truly was alone in a way that affected none of the others.

Pryderi looked warmly at the man who had been at his side for so long, and now was without family in an unfamiliar world, and said, 'The best friendship I can give shall be yours, if you want it. Come home with me. You will be welcome there.'

A decision was made in that moment that neither ever regretted. Pryderi and Manawydan returned to Dyfed together. Although the road was long, at last, like so many others before and after, they came home from their journey.

How joyful a warrior's homecoming after battle! How wonderful to see once more the familiar faces, familiar places – and how happy his wife and mother to see him safely returned, whether alone or in company.

Manawydan was grateful for the welcome and the fellowship offered to him as Pryderi's friend. Soon he would have cause to be grateful for more …

Pryderi and his wife Cigfa were reunited in a cascade of love and longing. Rhiannon of the Birds was overwhelmed with relief to see her son safe at home again. For Pryderi's sake she was ready to welcome his grizzled, battle-worn companion with all her heart.

However, when her eyes met those of Manawydan, she found to her astonishment that her heart welcomed him for her own sake, not as a mother, but as a woman. Those two, both well past the first flush of youth, and both long widowed, saw, looking into each other's eyes, someone to love and be loved by once more.

Not many days passed before Rhiannon spoke to her son and told him how she had found happiness with his companion. 'Pryderi, your friend Manawydan is an honourable man, and he and I have made an agreement to marry. After your father died, I did not believe I would ever meet another man whom I could love, but Manawydan has brought love back into my life and we are very happy. And by this sign you can know that it is true – my birds have come back to me once more.'

Sure enough, when Pryderi looked up, he saw the three birds circling her head and heard their familiar sweet song once more. He smiled. He was delighted to know that his mother and his friend loved each other as much as he loved them both, and he readily gave his blessing to their match.

So there was a wedding; and after the wedding a feast; and after the feast the two couples, Pryderi and Cigfa, and Rhiannon and Manawydan, set out on a circuit of the kingdom of Dyfed: to show the beauty of the land to Manawydan, to introduce him to its people, and to hunt and enjoy themselves together.

The storytellers of old say that when they wandered through the land they had never seen a more pleasant place, nor anywhere that was more abundant in all that was needed to live well.

During this time the two couples forged such a strong bond that not one of them wished to be parted from the other three. All was well, very well indeed.

And for a second time in this tale we have come to a place that could have been the moment of happy ever after. If only they had not …

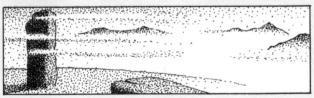

ne night, as the four of them feasted together at the high table in Pryderi's hall, their talk turned to the hill that could be seen from the windows, the magical mound called Gorsedd Arberth. Laughing, Pryderi pressed his mother to recount the old tale of how she had come riding towards that hill, out of her own world and into his father's world – and heart – while he, Pwyll, King of Dyfed, sat on the crown of the hill watching for a wonder.

'You see,' Rhiannon explained to Manawydan, 'it is said of that hill that if a person of noble birth sits at the top, not taking it lightly, but ready for whatever may befall, either he will receive blows and wounds or else he will see a wonder. Pryderi's father was not afraid of blows or wounds: he took the risk – and so we met.'

'And I came into this world, and so have good cause to be grateful to that hill and its magic!' laughed Pryderi.

'Does the magic still prevail?' asked Manawydan. 'Are there still wonders to be seen, by those who are not afraid to hazard everything?'

'I don't know,' replied Pryderi, and his face became solemn and thoughtful. 'In all the time since I inherited this throne, I have never made the attempt, never climbed the hill as my father did.'

'How could you?' asked his beloved, Cigfa. 'You were away after the war so long. Since you returned, you have barely had time to show the beauty of your kingdom to Manawydan, never mind try to awaken its magic.'

'Perhaps so,' replied Pryderi thoughtfully. 'But now there is nothing to stop me making the trial of my manhood there, as did my father before me. I have been tested as a king, and my people say that I rule well. I have been tested as a warrior, and have not been found wanting. However, I have yet to be tested by magic. I am not afraid of blows and wounds, and I should dearly like to see a wonder.' With these words, Pryderi rose decisively to his feet.

'You are going now?' asked Cigfa. But she did not expect an answer. Her husband's expression told her all she needed to know. 'Then I am coming with you! Whatever fate the hill sends you, I shall share it.'

Pryderi smiled at her, filled anew with love for her courage.

'And we will make the venture too,' said Rhiannon, rising from her place with Manawydan's hand in hers. 'We shall not be separated so soon, who have but lately learnt to rejoice in each other's company.'

Manawydan nodded. 'We will all come with you. Whatever magic the hill sends, whether for ease or trouble, we shall meet it together.'

With that, all four set out for the top of the hill. Climbing the magic mound, Pryderi's thoughts returned to the question his friend had asked while they still sat at the table, 'Does the magic of the hill still prevail?'

'We shall soon know,' he muttered to himself, as, with his family, he reached the crown of the hill. There, the companions stood shoulder to shoulder, to look out in the four directions at the beauty of Dyfed, bright with the light of the moon.

They had barely drawn breath, and turned their gaze on the land spread out before them, when the clash and clamour of some terrible noise besieged both hearing and vision. They swayed, overwhelmed by its intensity. As they did so, a thick grey mist came down, so suddenly that it was as though the moon were a candle which had been snuffed out. The land was hidden from their eyes.

Pryderi could not even see his own hand in front of his face, nor any sign of his wife and companions. He called out to them. His voice was swallowed by the mist, which filled his mouth and thickened his throat until his bold shout became a muffled mumble. He staggered, confused and afraid, aware that he was caught in some magic which was surely malevolent. He did not know how long this time of terror continued, only that, after a long time – or perhaps a short time – he blundered into a figure substantial to his touch. What is more, when he croaked hoarsely 'Who is there?', the reply came in the dear voice of his beloved Cigfa.

They clung to each other, while a sudden wind whipped at the mist and tore it into a travesty of triumphant pennants and flags. As the mist thickened in certain places, it thinned in others, and Pryderi made out the forms of the two other people he most longed to see: his mother and her consort. The four stumbled together, and clasped hands in a ring of certainty in this strangely shifting world.

As the mist cleared, Dyfed lay in front of them once more. But where before the land had been lit by moonlight, now it was bright as day, though the sun itself was not visible through the rising mist, which was like a morning heat haze. Something else was different too. The land was covered by forest. There was no sign of human life. Anywhere. Dyfed had returned to the wild.

Pryderi drew in his breath sharply, like a man bereaved. Even though it made no sense to ask, he did so anyway: 'What has happened?'

His companions were silent. They knew no more than he.

By the time they had descended the mound and returned to Pryderi's hall, they had part of the answer: no living being remained in or near the hall. They searched chamber and stable, but each opened door told the same story: no one else was there. They called the names of those they knew as well as their own family. No reply came. The four of them were alone in a land stripped of its people.

As this hit home, each retreated into a gloomy silence. They felt vulnerable. And they felt culpable, as human beings will. Pryderi blamed himself for overweening pride, which had led him to the top of the hill knowing it could equally bring good or ill, yet assuming that all would be well. Cigfa felt she had encouraged his foolhardiness by her readiness to accompany him. Rhiannon thought back anxiously over her life and recalled enemies from her Otherworld home, any one of whom had both the motive and the power to bring this disaster down on her family. Only Manawydan seemed able to keep his mind free of such paralysing guilt. Only Manawydan could see a way forward.

'We four must survive, to hold the royal line of Dyfed. We must live as though we believe that the people of the land will be restored, and hold the land in trust for them against that time.'

His words rang true, and they reached Pryderi through the lingering fog of his despair, 'My friend, you are right, and I am wrong to let myself lose hope. While the king lives, his duty is to the land. We must hold it until the people return.'

So, with Manawydan's words to kindle hope in his heart, Pryderi set his mind to the task of keeping his companions, and himself, alive.

It did not prove too difficult. At first they stayed close to the great hall, using up the stores there. After a while, they began to live on meat from the hunt and food foraged from the earth, as the ancestors had done for time immemorial. Though the land was empty of people and tame animals, the forest, they discovered, still teemed with wild beast and fowl, and the rivers with fish. They found a closer connection to the land through living from its bounty.

But as the days passed and turned to weeks, and the weeks to months, Pryderi began to weary of the simple thing his life had become, and to long for action once more.

Manawydan saw his frustration, and thought long and hard about what might be done to alleviate it. One day, he said to Pryderi, 'Why do we not travel eastwards, into Lloegr, which is also called England, to search for human companionship and a way to earn a living, instead of wresting it from the land?'

Pryderi was ready and eager for a new adventure. Rhiannon and Cigfa declared that they too would welcome a change. So the four companions set out.

England! What could the hero of a Welsh tale be doing there? Why did Pryderi's journey take him so far from his home?

After his own country had become a wasteland, what else were he and his family to do, but become strangers in a strange land?

Once they had crossed into England, Pryderi turned to his companion and counsellor, his stepfather Manawydan. 'How are we to live?' he asked.

'By our own efforts, how else?' replied the pragmatist. 'I am skilled in making saddles. I can show you how. It is an honourable trade. We shall be saddle makers.'

So they went to Hereford, and set up in business. They prospered. Manawydan had spoken truly: he was so skilled in the craft, and such a good teacher, that soon their saddles were judged the finest for miles around, and no one would buy from anyone else. It was not long before the saddle makers of the town became jealous and suspicious of these incomers to their place and to their market. They began to talk of setting on the interlopers and driving them away.

When word reached Pryderi that the saddle makers were plotting against them, intending to kill or oust them, he was ready to fight to defend his family. But Manawydan, older and wiser, counselled otherwise, 'We have taken their trade and their livelihood. It is not fair to them. We should just move on.'

Pryderi protested, but the women also preferred peace. Rhiannon and Cigfa were in agreement with Manawydan. Pryderi knew that their counsel was wise, and so he listened to them. The time he had spent living close to the land and learning the wisdom of nature had made him less headstrong than he had been in his youth, more ready to be advised.

So they left that place and found another town and another trade.

'We can be shield makers,' said Manawydan. 'I have the skill. I will teach the rest of you. It is an honourable way to make a living.'

They started a new project. Once again they prospered. They did so well that it was not long before their shields had become the most popular in the marketplace, and the other shield makers of the town found their business dwindling.

Once again threats of violence were made against Pryderi and his family. Once again Pryderi was ready to fight, a shield of his own making on his arm. But a second time Manawydan's words showed him the other side of the argument. 'They were here before us. It would be better for them, and for us, if we were to go somewhere else.'

Once more Pryderi listened to his advice. Once more the exiles moved on. When they were settled, Pryderi turned to Manawydan. 'How shall we live this time?'

They became shoemakers. To Pryderi, it did not seem as honourable a trade as making the weapons of a warrior or the accoutrements of a rider, but it met a need. Their shoes were well made, and they soon became the most sought-after shoemakers in the place. So, of course, the other shoemakers conspired against them.

'I am sick of this,' cried Pryderi. 'Let us at least defend ourselves against these threats!'

'No,' said Manawydan. 'It would be better for them if we left them their livelihood. It would be better for us to go home.'

How much they longed, all four, to see their own land once more. They were suddenly overwhelmed by *hiraeth*, a nostalgic, melancholic longing for home. It is so peculiarly Welsh an emotion, that no single English word can express its full meaning.

'Yes,' said Rhiannon, 'Let us go home – to Dyfed.'

The road was long, but the tale can be short. At last they found themselves once more in their own place. It was still empty of people, but wild animals were plentiful. So they began to live from the land again, the women gathering food as women have done since the earliest times, and the two men hunting. Soon Pryderi and Manawydan had a pack of hounds trained as well as any of the hunting hounds of Pryderi's court had been. With these they would go out every day, creating for themselves a simple routine to meet the necessities of life, which they imagined nothing could shatter.

How wrong they were! The magic, which had utterly changed their land, was still at work. Its unknown possessor was waiting to wreak havoc upon their lives once more.

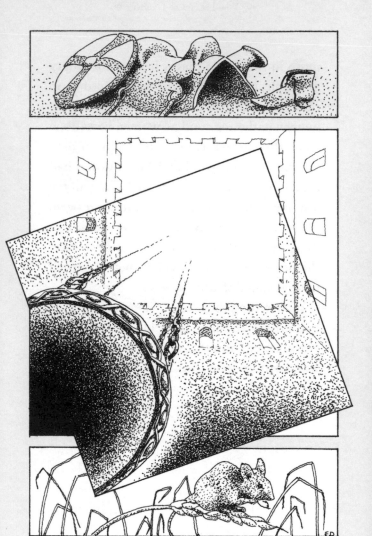

ne day, as Pryderi and Manawydan hunted, their hounds raised a pure white boar, with red tips to its ears and angry red eyes. They had never seen such a wonderful creature. The hounds were terrified and shrank from the beast, but the two men urged them on, until at last they charged. The boar held the hounds at bay, but little by little retreated from the hunters. Eagerly Pryderi and Manawydan followed their quarry, not realising that it was drawing them deeper and deeper into the forest.

Then they saw before them a great grey castle. It stood in a place they knew well, a place where nothing had been before. The boar disappeared inside. The hunters stopped, but the hounds, now strangely eager, raced in after their prey. Pryderi and Manawydan were motionless, staring at this mysterious evidence of the work of human – or superhuman? – hands. Only little by little did they become aware that neither the belling of the hounds nor the snorting of the boar could any longer be heard. The place was as silent and still as if nothing had ever disturbed its stones. The two men waited for their dogs to return, but not one came out through the wide-open gates. At last Manawydan turned away. But Pryderi would not move.

'I will not abandon my dogs,' he said.

'We should not go in,' warned Manawydan. 'Whoever put the spell on the land surely sent the boar and raised this castle. There is dark magic here.'

Certainly Manawydan was right. But Pryderi would not listen to him. Stepping over the threshold of an enchanted castle in the forest is not a prudent act! But Pryderi, whose name means 'anxiety' or 'care', could still be, in spite of all the teaching that life had brought him, a man whose nature meant he did not think overmuch about the consequences of his actions, or how they might impact on those who loved him. Ignoring Manawydan's warnings of magic and danger, and determined not to lose his dogs, he went into the stronghold.

He found himself in an empty courtyard surrounded by high walls, with a well at the centre. The well was encircled by marble slabs, and above it, suspended from four chains reaching away and out of sight, up into the very sky itself, hung a golden bowl. The bowl was of marvellous workmanship, intricately decorated and beautiful to see, but something beyond its appearance enchanted Pryderi. He simply could not help reaching out to it.

As soon as his hands touched the bowl, its magic held him. Unable to move, speak, or call for help, he was fixed there, as silent and still as a statue.

Outside the castle, in the forest, Manawydan waited for him. And waited. He saw no sign of Pryderi or the hounds he had followed into that place; nor indeed of the magical boar which had lured them all there. When darkness began to fall, Manawydan at last gave up his vigil and returned home, where Rhiannon and Cigfa were waiting. When they saw him coming back alone they were filled with foreboding.

'Where is your companion? Where are the dogs?' Rhiannon's voice was sharp with anxiety. He told as much of the story as he knew and, as she listened, Rhiannon's face darkened with fear and anger.

'A poor friend you have been!' she cried shrilly, and ran out into the forest to search for her son. Manawydan and Cigfa called out, trying to stop her, warning her of the danger and the magic. She paid no heed. She found her way straight to the magical castle, almost as though her feet were drawn along the path which led there. The gates were open, and she rushed in. Inside, she saw Pryderi, quite still, his hands clasping a golden bowl of great beauty, which hung from chains stretching up into the sky.

'My son,' she gasped, 'what has happened to you here?'

He didn't move or speak. His eyes held a mute warning, but she did not stop to read it. She ran to him, as any mother would, and reached out to draw his hands away from the bowl. As soon as she touched it, she too was held fast by its magic. Frozen and mute, mother and son stared at each other across the enchanted bowl. Then mist swirled around them, a great noise deafened them, and the castle, with them inside it, was gone: out of this world, out of time.

The magic of the castle took Pryderi and Rhiannon out of their own world, dumb, motionless and helpless as they were. As they stood like statues, a figure came towards them through the mist. They saw a man in a long grey cloak. His face was twisted into a triumphant, sneering smile.

He said, 'All that you have been through, since long before you mounted the magical mound, has come about because of my curse on you. Now I have you at my mercy. But you will have no mercy from me,

Pryderi, for your father and mother showed none to my friend and kinsman, my blood brother ...'

Then his voice changed, and lost its harsh, crowing edge. It became softer, though still sinister. 'But perhaps you do not know who I am. Your mother, however, will remember me, I think. I am Llwyd, the Grey Lord.'

Rhiannon drew in her breath sharply at the name, but no alarm could show on her frozen face. Their captor turned to her. 'You, Rhiannon, plotted shame and humiliation on the man who was betrothed to you: you rejected him, a man of our world, for the father of this young pup – a mere human!'

Rhiannon looked at Pryderi. Pryderi looked at Rhiannon. He remembered the story she had told him, of his parents' wedding feast, of the unwelcome suitor whose place his father had taken. He searched his memory for the man's name. Rhiannon could not speak, the magic upon her, but her lips silently formed that name: Gwawl.

'Yes,' said the Grey Lord, 'Gwawl: he loved you, yet you rejected him. You and your puny human husband debased him, humbled him in front of his own people and yours, and then forced him to swear never to take revenge on you or your family. Perhaps you thought you had outwitted him. But things are not so simple. I have undertaken to punish you, on his behalf. I did not give my word, though I was there and saw it all. There are ties of blood and kinship between Gwawl and me, and I have vowed to avenge him. I have followed your fates, yours and your son's. I have sniffed the two of you out, wherever you went, all these long years. I am the root of all your troubles, the source of all your woes. And now I have you, under my control: in my realm, outside time. And I shall keep you at my pleasure. You will both remain here, trapped, for as long as I wish. And I have a fitting punishment for each of you, to remind you, as you linger here, of the paths that brought you into my power.

'You, Rhiannon, will be made to wear the collars of my horses about your neck, to remind you of your long years beside the mounting block, carrying travellers on your back like a packhorse: the punishment you suffered after your baby was stolen … stolen by my creature, my craft. And you, Pryderi, will have the hammers of my gates hung round your neck, to remind you of your foolishness in rushing into my castle, and so into my power and under my enchantment.'

With that, he disappeared, and Pryderi and Rhiannon were left to languish between the worlds, trapped outside time.

What of those they had left behind? Pryderi's wife, Cigfa, and Manawydan, Rhiannon's husband, had to find a way to live with despair. They waited and waited for their loved ones, but of course, neither came back. When they went out to search, the castle was gone, as if it had never been. There were no glad voices carried on the breeze, no sounds of family coming home;

even the birds seemed hushed, and the forest foreboding.

Cigfa began to weep, pale and scared, but Manawydan comforted her. 'Don't be afraid; I will take care of you. I will be like a father to you, and keep you safe from harm, until your husband returns to you, and my wife to me. We must live as though they will return. Indeed, we must *believe* they will return, and keep the fire burning and our hearts open for them, to make sure that they do!'

Cigfa swallowed her sobs, scrubbed the tears from her cheeks and squared her shoulders. 'You are right,' she said, 'I am weak-hearted to give up hope. We must carry on living.'

So they continued, just the two, chastely sharing the little bothy they had built while they were still four. They hunted, they foraged, they worked, and they survived in that wild enchanted land. Until, one day, Manawydan said, 'I have had enough of living as a hunter. I want to turn my hand to farming – I want to plant corn, and grow wheat to mill flour, so that we can bake bread once more. Let us go to barter for seed corn in the markets of England.'

So they went away once again, to the part of the world where real life obtained and magic was distant, spoken of only in stories. There they traded skins and pelts for tools to till the earth and seed to plant in it.

They came back with enough seed to plant three fields of wheat. The ground was rich and fertile; the wheat was of good stock. It sprouted well. Soon they had three fields of bright green shoots which put down strong and healthy roots. The weather blessed them, the sun bleaching the stalks and ripening the ears to a good golden glow. The wheat grew tall and rippled in the breeze. The ears became heavy. Manawydan strode through his fields like a farmer, checking the weather, estimating his yield, muttering about pests.

Then, one evening, he came home and said to Cigfa, 'The first field is ready. Where's that sickle? I'll sharpen it now, to be ready at dawn to reap our first harvest.'

True to his word, he set out at sunrise with the smooth-bladed sickle in his hand, eager to gather the first fruits of his work. But when he reached his land he stared in disbelief: the field had been stripped bare. Not a single ear of wheat was to be seen, only the bare stalks, snapped off at half their height, rattling in the wind in a travesty of the smooth sound that the ripening ears had made as they rustled against each other. Manawydan cast about for some sign of what had happened, slashed to and fro impotently with the sickle, walked the whole boundary of the field looking for clues, and at last came back to Cigfa hot, cross and dejected.

'I cannot guess what happened,' he told her, 'for there is no one else within miles, as we both know well, yet I cannot think of any beast that could have done this.' He shook his head, baffled and downhearted.

But Manawydan was not a man to allow life to defeat him for long. Soon his smile returned, and he said to Cigfa, 'The second sowing is ready now, too. I could have cut it today, if I had not wasted so much time fretting about the first field. I will harvest our second field in the morning.'

So, heartening himself, he slept, and set out in the morning to his meadow. But the second field, which only the day before had been a golden sea of ripe wheat, had been reduced to a dusty expanse of pale, spiked stubble. There was no sign of Manawydan's crop, nor of the one who had stolen it.

He returned to Cigfa pale-faced and furious, unable to find the words to express himself. She puzzled away with him at what might be the cause, until he lost patience with her as well as himself, and stormed away to fulminate against nothing in particular and everything in general at the edge of his third and final field. But Manawydan was a moderate man, and soon enough, sense prevailed.

He came back to Cigfa, apologising for his behaviour, and told her what he had decided to do. 'I cannot lose the last of the crop, after all the work we have put into it. Even though the other two are gone, this one remaining field could see us through the worst of the winter, if only I can protect it and bring our harvest home. I dare not fail again: if I do, we have lost everything.'

Cigfa encouraged him. 'You will not fail. I'm sure it will be well. What have you decided to do?'

It was obvious from the set of his jaw that he had come to a decision. 'I'll sit up tonight and keep watch over the field. Whoever is stealing our grain will not catch me unawares a third time.' With that, he set aside the sickle and sharpened his sword instead.

The day passed slowly. At last night fell. Cigfa saw him off to the field, and settled down to wait for him to return.

Long before morning came, unable to sleep, she was stirring the embers of the fire into life. She heard him coming back. She turned her head at the sound of Manawydan's triumphant voice.

'I have caught the thief – or one of them at least! I have it here.'

She looked at a bunched glove, hanging from his upraised fist. 'What kind of thief would fit in your glove?' she asked.

'A mouse. The theft was committed by an army of mice; this is the one I have caught and this is the one I will punish.'

Cigfa looked dubiously at the small bundle in his hand, but made no further comment on it. 'Tell me what happened,' was all she said.

'Picture a wheat field,' began Manawydan, eager to tell his tale, to share the memory as vividly as possible.

'Picture the moon. Picture silver light on a golden swathe of grain. Picture a farmer, crouched beside his field, keeping watch for thieves with his naked sword across his knees. It's me, protecting the crop, the fruit of all our work, the promise of food for you and me.

Time passes. Nothing happens. Time passes. I'm dozing. I jerk awake, only to doze again. Then, in the very darkest part of the night, the wheat ripples. But there is no wind. The stalks rustle. But there is nothing there.'

'I'm alert now; I leap to my feet, straining my senses for any sight or sound of the thief! After a moment or two, I become aware of a scurrying … a grey, furry, scrabbling, tailed, toothed, clawed army of … mice! More mice than I have ever seen before: hundreds of mice, thousands of mice, one for every ear of wheat. Each mouse climbs a stalk and bites through an ear, to carry off our hard-earned harvest. Well, I leap in amongst them, sword in hand, chasing them … but have you ever tried to catch a mouse? It's easier said than done. So it isn't long before I throw down the sword and begin to leap here and there … but they are so swift! I think every single one is going to get away, until I spot one which is a bit fatter, a bit slower than any of the others. I go after that one – I snatch at it and scoop

it up. I catch it! But I don't know what to
do with it, until I remember my glove folded
over my belt. So I pull out the glove, shake it
out and drop the mouse in. And here it is!'

Cigfa looked at the struggling, wriggling,
desperate bundle. 'And what will you do
with it, now you have caught it?'

'I will hang it at dawn.'

Her response was simple. 'That's foolish.
You can't hang a mouse.'

'I can and I will,' said Manawydan, clos-
ing the open end of the glove by tying a cord
around it. Then he hung it, with his small
prisoner inside, from a peg in the wall. 'If I
had been able to catch them all I would have
hanged the lot of them. Having only this one,
it will suffer for them all.'

Cigfa sighed, but she did not pursue the
matter.

However, with the morning light, she
was up and ready before Manawydan. He
knew better than to question her obvious
determination to come with him, to witness

what she clearly saw as foolish caprice on his part. She followed him from their little hut and, to her surprise, they began to climb Gorsedd Arberth.

'This magical mound is where all our troubles began,' reflected Cigfa ruefully, as she followed the determined figure of Manawydan to the top. There he put down the captive mouse in its glove-prison, and began to tie twigs together.

Cigfa asked, 'What are you doing?'

Manawydan merely replied, 'I am building the gallows from which to hang the thief.'

Cigfa forbore to enquire further, tucking her skirts around her as she settled herself on the grassy knoll and turned her head away, to gaze with apparent tranquility out over the land which she once had ruled as queen.

Manawydan worked quickly and deftly at his self-appointed task, but before he had completed it, a figure came up over the brow of the hill towards them. It was a mendicant friar, dressed in a simple habit and

carrying a begging bowl. Cigfa was astonished to see a stranger, after they had lived
so long in the kingdom without sight or sign
of anyone apart from their own four-fold
family. Manawydan, however, was absorbed
in his intricate task, and greeted the stranger
absent-mindedly, as though members of the
clergy passed by every day.

'I greet you in return, sir,' responded the
friar. 'But may I ask what you are about?'

'I am building a gallows to hang a thief,'
responded Manawydan politely.

'What thief could be small enough to be
hanged on such a structure?' asked the stranger.

'The thief is a mouse,' replied Manawydan.

'Sir, it demeans your dignity to deal with
such a creature,' said the friar. 'Would it not
be better to let the animal go?'

'No,' replied Manawydan, sitting back
on his heels to look full at the friar for
the first time. 'The mouse is a thief and it
deserves the punishment decreed by law. It
will hang.'

The friar reached into his begging bowl. 'There is a golden coin here. I offer it to you in exchange for the life of the mouse.'

'I will not take it,' replied Manawydan.

'Sir, it is not fitting to your status for you to deal with such a creature, but if you will neither sell it nor let it go …'

'I will not,' interrupted Manawydan.

'Then I must leave you to continue your business,' said the friar, and he walked away down the mound and out of sight.

Manawydan began to fix the crosspiece to his construction. Another figure came into sight. It was a priest in a plain and sober garment. Manawydan seemed oblivious to his presence, until the stranger greeted him and asked, 'Sir, what are you doing?'

'I am building a gallows to hang a thief.'

'It is a very small gallows,' observed the priest.

'It is a very small thief,' responded Manawydan, 'but a guilty one nonetheless. It is a mouse.'

'A man of status, as you yourself seem to be, should not demean himself by handling such a creature. Why not let it go?'

'I will not,' replied Manawydan stubbornly.

'Let me offer you three golden coins in exchange for its life, for it would be more seemly for you to release it than to handle it.'

'The life of the mouse is not for sale,' replied Manawydan drily, 'and the punishment laid down by law is not to be bought off.'

'Sir, I had no intention to offend you. Do as you see fit,' murmured the priest, pocketing the coins he had proffered and turning away down the hill.

Scarcely had he gone, than a procession of laden packhorses plodded up the hill, accompanying a man dressed in the luxurious fur-lined robe of a bishop. Manawydan was busily engaged in twisting thread into a noose to string up on his little crossbeam.

'Good day to you, sir,' said the bishop. 'May I ask what you are making there?'

'It is a gallows to hang a thief, which is a mouse, which I will not free for silver or gold,' replied Manawydan, scarcely bothering to look up from his work.

'I will offer you seven gold coins for its life,' said the bishop.

'I will not take them.'

'I will offer you the loads of my seven pack-horses, and the beasts themselves besides.'

'I will not take them.'

'Sir, what do you want for the life of that mouse?'

Manawydan looked full into the face of the stranger for the first time. 'I want my wife, Rhiannon, and her son, Pryderi, returned safely home to us.'

Cigfa turned at this, looking closely at Manawydan's determined face, then at the richly dressed stranger. Who was he?

The outsider spoke, 'You shall have that. Let the mouse go.'

'I will not, unless I see the magic lifted from this land, and the kingdom of Dyfed restored and all its people returned to their former state.'

'You shall have that too. Let the mouse go.'

'I will not, without a solemn promise that no curse or vengeance will fall from anywhere on me or Pryderi or Rhiannon or Cigfa, or any future generation of our family.'

'You have set a clever and cunning condition,' spat the stranger, 'for otherwise a curse would have followed your line to the seventh generation. But it will beset you no more. On this you have my solemn word, for I must save the life of the mouse. Now let it go.'

'I will not, until I see Rhiannon and Pryderi coming up the hill towards us,' said Manawydan, his hand tight around the glove, inside which was the mouse.

'You shall have that,' said the man in the rich robe.

Cigfa looked wildly then in all directions, and saw them – her husband, coming back to her, his mother's hand in his. As far as she could tell, the two of them were whole and unharmed. She leapt to her feet and ran down the hill and into Pryderi's outstretched arms, laughing and crying and calling his name all in the same gulping, gasping breath.

Manawydan, however, did not move or stand or turn. His eyes were locked on those of his adversary, who said, yet again, 'Let the mouse go.'

'Not until you tell me why its life is so important to you, and what has been happening here.'

The stranger sighed, and shrugged off his heavy outer garment. Beneath it, he wore a long grey cloak. There was a sharp intake of breath from Rhiannon. However, though she stood now at his side, Manawydan ignored her, keeping his eyes fixed on the stranger's face.

'I am Llwyd, the Grey Lord. I come from the Otherworld, and I am kinsman and blood brother to Gwawl. He is the man who was insulted and rejected by this woman, your wife, and her first husband. Rhiannon is nearly as cunning as you, sir, and bound Gwawl with a solemn promise against using magic or mystery to wreak vengeance for his slighting and loss. But no such vow bound me, so I decided to set to work to avenge my friend.'

'All that Rhiannon and her son have suffered these long years since that day has its beginning and ending in me. This young woman,' he continued, pointing to Cigfa, still in Pryderi's embrace, 'fell foul of me too, as indeed did you yourself, once you bound your fates with theirs. But when you turned farmer, you changed the game, and now it is I who am at your mercy.'

'How so?' asked Manawydan, rising at last to put his arm around Rhiannon's shoulders.

'When your fields were ripe, I changed my people into mice, to steal the wheat ears and ruin your hopes and spoil your harvest. At first, I sent only my warriors and lords. But the women of the court heard the tales of their adventures in your first fields, and they wanted to take part in the sport. At last I agreed to change their shapes too. My wife would not be left out and insisted that I set the shape-changing spell on her, although she is expecting our first child. This I did, against my judgment, for love of her. Because of that one mistake, you have won this chance to bargain with me.

'Being big with child, she was slow and heavy, and so, alone out of all my people, she was the one you were able to catch last night. She is the mouse you now hold captive in your glove. I love her, and cannot risk losing her, or our unborn child. All that you have asked for I concede, for love of her and in fear for her life. Now that your wife and her son have been returned to you, set mine free. Break up the gallows you have made, and release my wife.'

Manawydan looked around, and Rhiannon, at his side, slowly nodded her head. Then she spoke. 'This foolish game of retribution and revenge can be stopped here, at last, if only we show mercy, as Llwyd has not ... I too did wrong, when I urged my first husband to trick Gwawl so long ago, and so began this senseless round.

Manawydan, help me right that wrong and bring an end to all this cruelty. Set the mouse free.'

Cigfa too, who had been his only companion for so long, looked Manawydan in the eye. 'You vowed to keep me safe from harm until my husband should return, and you bid me keep faith that he would,' she said. 'You were right to keep hope in your heart, and without you I would not have survived. You are a good man. Show mercy. Let the mouse go.'

Manawydan reached down and picked up the glove. He pulled off the cord holding it closed, and shook the mouse out onto the ground. A moment later, a young woman stood there, her hands cupped protectively around her swollen belly.

She stepped towards Llwyd. He swept his cloak around her and turned away without a word. Hip to hip, the two walked away down the side of the hill, and as they did so they melted and vanished from sight – as did the packhorses, their loads, the bishop's robe discarded on the ground, and all trace of Llwyd's malign spell.

As Llwyd disappeared forever out of their lives and stories, Pryderi and his family looked down from the top of the mound and saw the kingdom restored to its former abundance. Smoke rose from the homesteads, beasts grazed in the meadows, farmers tilled their fields, mothers shooed their children out from under their feet, or called them in from the gardens. Pryderi turned and smiled at his family, and they smiled back, their faces unshadowed by trouble or care.

Then, hand in hand in hand in hand, the four came down the magical mound, to their home, their lives and their contentment. The Birds of Rhiannon swooped down, as if from nowhere, to circle about them, and they laughed with the joy of it.

Once more they could be happy and live in peace.

After this, many years of peace and plenty passed in Pryderi's kingdom, and all the trials he had suffered, if not forgotten, faded in memory until they seemed distant. His land flourished, his people lived happily and all was well. The farmers followed Manawydan's lead and began to plant wheat. They kept hens and geese, raised sheep and cattle. They became the first people in any of the kingdoms of the land to keep domestic pigs, eschewing the wild boar which were so dangerous to hunt, and too tough to be toothsome.

Such peaceful interludes are precious indeed, but stories skate swiftly past them, concentrating instead on trouble and turmoil. The old tellers of this tale leave no word of how Pryderi and Cigfa spent their days during this long peaceful period; whether they had children; or how Rhiannon and Manawydan fared as they grew old.

However, Pryderi's story shows that he had the friendship of the King of the Otherworld, because of the ties of blood through his mother's line that linked him to that world.

The Otherworld king sent gifts, just as he had done in Pryderi's father's time. One of the most precious of these presents, given to Pryderi's father and still treasured under Pryderi's rule, was a new and rich source of food: animals which were easy to feed and pleasant to eat; animals which had never been seen in this world before. These animals, so valuable and so rare, were nothing more nor less than pigs, but they have an important role to play in the conclusion of Pryderi's story.

It began well enough, as Pryderi welcomed to his court bards from the court of Math, King of Gwynedd in North Wales. He was a successor to the giant king, Bran, whose dynasty had been wiped out in the wars in which Pryderi had fought. Math was a mighty magician as well as a great king, and his fame had certainly travelled as far south as Dyfed, to reach Pryderi's ears.

The bards were greeted as ambassadors. Their leaders were two brothers, nephews of their king, named Gilfaethwy and Gwydion. Gwydion came dressed in the robes of a bard, and the tale tells that he was the best story-teller in the world. However, he was also a powerful sorcerer. He had come to Pryderi's court with a secret aim, and this was to stir up trouble between the Northern and Southern kingdoms by trickery and magic.

Pryderi knew nothing of this. He welcomed the bards in good faith. A feast was prepared, and places of honour were set at the high table, one to each side of Pryderi, for their two leaders. It was a fine feast, and they ate and drank the best of everything. When at last the plates were empty and the bellies were full, the servers moved around the hall to replenish the goblets one more time, and then all eyes turned expectantly to the high table, where the bards sat.

Pryderi spoke to Gwydion. 'Sir,' he said, 'will you give us a story? Will you tell us a tale?'

'That I will gladly,' replied Gwydion.

So Pryderi and the people of his court sat late into the night listening to Gwydion's tales: the stories that were already old while Pryderi's was still unfolding. They were all swept up in the magic of the words and the music of the voice of that accomplished storyteller. When all others had retired to sleep, their thoughts and dreams full of images from the stories, Pryderi and Gwydion remained by the fire, deep in conversation.

'My Lord,' asked Gwydion, 'could anyone put my request to you better than I myself can?'

'Indeed, no,' replied Pryderi. 'You have already proved your skills with the spoken word. What is in your mind?'

'I have come to ask for some of the marvellous animals that were sent as gifts to you by the Lord of the Otherworld. We have heard great things in the North about the fine flavour of their flesh.'

'The creatures are called pigs,' replied Pryderi, 'and it is true that until my father received them from the Otherworld they had never been seen in our world before. If the decision were mine alone I would willingly give you some, but I have promised my people that I will neither sell nor give away a single beast until our herd has doubled in size.'

'I see,' said Gwydion. 'Yet there may be a way you can help me without breaking your word. Do not give me the pigs, but do not refuse me either. Tomorrow I will offer you an exchange for them, so that you will lose neither face nor wealth.'

After agreeing to speak further the next day, they parted: Pryderi to his chambers, and Gwydion to his lodgings, where the members of his party were waiting anxiously to know whether he had persuaded Pryderi to hand over the pigs.

The pigs were very important to them. To Gwydion and his brother, the pigs were much more than a source of food. They were part of a plan, hatched by Gwydion, which had nothing to do with the wishes or commands of King Math of Gwynedd. Gwydion and his band were not in Pryderi's kingdom at the command of their king. He did not even know they were there. Gwydion was on a personal, and dangerous, mission.

Gwydion's aim was to help his brother, Gilfaethwy, gain access to a woman with whom he had become utterly besotted, a beautiful maiden in the court of King Math. The king's fate required him to sit always, unless the country went to war, with his feet in the lap of a maiden. The only time King Math would ever be apart from this maiden was if he went to war – anywhere, for any fight. And this maiden was the one who was the object of Gilfaethwy's obsession. Gwydion was determined to stir up trouble between Pryderi and Math, set their two kingdoms at war, and send Math out onto the battlefield, so that Gilfaethwy might sneak into the court and find the maiden alone and undefended. The pigs had been picked as the perfect provocation.

It seems that neither Gwydion nor Gilfaethwy had thought through what the consequences of their acts might be. They put their desires above any other consideration, and this caused great suffering.

'As he has refused to give you the pigs, shall we take them by force?' asked Gilfaethwy breathlessly.

'Indeed, no,' replied Gwydion. 'We do not want his wrath turned against us here. And you are wrong. He has not refused. Brother, you are altogether too hot-headed – as indeed we all know, for otherwise we should not be here, pandering to your passions. We certainly do not want to bring trouble down upon our heads here. We must return to the North, and draw him after us. Otherwise, all this subterfuge will be in vain.'

'Listen to my plan: I shall make an exchange with him, offering such wonderful animals that he will be eager to trade the pigs. But I will create the gifts we shall barter by magic, and they will not endure for long: long enough for us to get away, but not so long that we risk him losing our trail. He will be angered by the deception, and he will pursue us. We will draw him after us and lead him into a trap. We will send word ahead to King Math, warning him that the army of the South is on the march. Then Math in turn will arm against them. So trouble will brew, and the two war bands will fight. And while Pryderi and Math battle it out, you, dear brother, shall be free to spend time with the maiden of your dreams.' Gwydion burst into laughter.

Gilfaethwy stared at him, caught between admiration for his brother's cunning, and loathing at having become utterly reliant upon it to gain his desire. 'What, then, will you make with your magic?' he asked in a strangled voice.

'You'll see,' replied Gwydion shortly. 'And so will he, come the morning. Now leave me. I have much to do.'

All night Gwydion worked his magic. He was a great sorcerer and shape-changer, and to put the form of one thing onto something else was not hard for him. From a heap of damp toadstools he created horses and hounds, the finest ever seen. He made a dozen of each: long-limbed hunting horses equipped with saddles and bridles; bright-eyed dogs with collars and leashes; all their accoutrements of the finest workmanship, all of gold.

The next morning, well pleased with his work, he brought the creatures he had made to the court. Pryderi looked at the fine beasts, and his eyes shone.

'Take these in exchange for your pigs, my lord,' urged Gwydion. 'This way, your promise will remain unbroken, for you will have neither sold nor given them away.'

Pryderi considered the matter for a while, but in truth he was soon persuaded. Suspecting nothing, and believing that Gwydion was as trustworthy as he seemed and sounded, he agreed to the exchange. So it was made.

Pryderi's new horses were taken to the stables, their beautiful saddles and bridles carefully stored. The hounds went to the kennels, the collars left about their necks and the leashes coiled upon a shelf. Pryderi wandered from stables to kennels and back again, admiring the animals. He lounged lazily against the stable door and whispered to the horses.

Gwydion, in contrast, was all bustle and business. He needed to get away before his deceit was discovered. He drove the pigs before him to the place where his party waited, horses already saddled, everything packed up, ready for a hard ride.

'Now we must go as swiftly as we may!' cried Gwydion. 'The magic will hold only for a day.' They set off northwards, taking care to get a good lead, while still leaving enough of a trail to lure Pryderi after them.

The next morning, Pryderi woke early, and straightaway his thoughts turned to his new horses. His connection with the animals remained strong, though it was a long time since he had been parted from the stallion which had been his boyhood companion. More than the hounds, splendid though they were, the horses called to him, and he was eager to ride the one he had picked out for himself.

But when he reached the stables where the new horses had been housed, there was nothing there. He called to the grooms, who came running, but they were as puzzled as he. It was the same story at the kennels. The animals – and their trappings – had completely disappeared.

Pryderi could not make sense of what had happened, but his instincts told him that, yet again, some powerful and magical force was opposing him. Into his mind flashed a story he had almost forgotten: the memory of his foster-father's two years of trouble, before he vanquished a monster and found a baby in the shadows. He remembered listening to Teyrnon's tale of going into his stable on May Day morning, two years running, only to find, both times, that his newborn foal had vanished overnight. 'Is that story to be lived through yet again?' Pryderi wondered.

At last, though, the truth became clear: his horses and hounds had not been stolen. They had, indeed, simply disappeared, though not quite into thin air. Rather, they and their leads, collars, saddles and bridles had once more become the toadstools from which Gwydion had conjured them, and which now were to be found, stinking and rotting, in the corners of the kennels and the stables, as well as on every shelf. They were all that was left in the aftermath of Gwydion's magic.

Furious and insulted, Pryderi raised his war band and set out in pursuit, to seek redress for the affront and trickery of Gwydion. It was not difficult to track the fleeing riders, driving the pigs before them. Gwydion had taken pains to leave plenty of signs along their way, to make sure that Pryderi did not lose the trail. However, he and his men kept enough of a lead to

ensure that Pryderi would not catch up with
them too soon, while their small group still
remained isolated and vulnerable. They
headed for home: the kingdom of Gwynedd,
where they would have the protection of
their king and his warriors. Pryderi pursued
them, against the advice of his companions-
at-arms, into enemy territory, where he and
his men would be the ones at risk.

Gwydion made sure that they would
receive a hostile reception, by spinning
tales of guile to his own king, taking him in
with his plausible words as easily as he had
deceived Pryderi. 'Lord, Pryderi of Dyfed has
pursued us the length of the land with one
aim in view: to cause trouble here in your
kingdom. He treated us with great discour-
tesy in his own realm, and now seeks to make
mischief here. I urge you to prepare to fight,
for he is bloodthirsty, well-armed and unwill-
ing to listen to reason.'

Accordingly, having no reason to mis-
trust Gwydion's words, Math raised his

war band. When Pryderi and his followers reached the Northern kingdom, Math's
army was waiting for them. Gwydion
was amongst the leaders. Meanwhile his
brother Gilfaethwy, obsessed with thoughts
of the maiden who, until then, had held
the king's feet in her lap, remained behind
at court so that he might take her, without
ever wondering what her wishes might be
in the matter.

Battle was joined, and both sides suffered great loss, until Pryderi was forced to
retreat. The opposing army followed, and
more were slaughtered. After this, Pryderi
rallied his men, consulted with his advisors,
and sent a messenger to King Math under a
flag of truce.

'This matter is not of my making,' was
the word Pryderi sent to Math. 'It was your
nephew Gwydion who came uninvited to my
land, where he treated me falsely. He took
the precious beasts I agreed to trade with
him, but left in exchange nothing but worth-

less fakeries of magic, which melted into mushrooms when the light of day fell on them. For this reason I pursued him, seeking the return of my own goods, and for this reason only I brought my warriors under war banner to your land.

'My quarrel is with Gwydion alone. I would not see one hair harmed nor any further drop of blood shed by any man here, whether of my war band or of yours. Let this matter be settled between Gwydion and me in single combat, sword to sword and shield to shield. It is only fair that the man who has done me this wrong should set his body against mine.'

The messenger fell silent and bowed low. His words and manner pleased Math, who acknowledged Pryderi's courage to himself. He said, 'I will not force a battle risking many lives, if it can be prevented in this way.'

All then turned to Gwydion, to know his response to the challenge. 'I will not ask the men of Gwynedd to die on my behalf, when

I can fight Pryderi, man to man. I will set my body against his gladly,' replied Gwydion.

These sounded like the brave words of a warrior, but in fact he knew that he would vanquish Pryderi by sorcery and magic, being no match for him in strength or valour. And whether Pryderi had learnt this from his first encounter with Gwydion, the story does not say.

The opposing armies gathered at a place where two rivers met, forming up on opposite sides of the flood plain, leaving space between them for the duel to the death. There they stood, ready to watch the combat between Pryderi and Gwydion. Many were relieved beyond words that they themselves were spared any more part in the fighting.

Speedily the tale is spun, but with less speed the deed is done, so the storytellers of old say. There is no easy way to describe what happened.

Pryderi and Gwydion faced each other, swords held high, shields at the ready. As soon as the signal was given, they rushed together and their weapons clashed; between the hushed armies they struck and blocked, slashed and lunged. To those who watched, they seemed equally matched, but in fact, though Pryderi was the better warrior, Gwydion had greater power, for he wielded Otherworldy magic which no mortal man could match.

By magic and enchantment, Gwydion forced Pryderi gradually back towards the riverbank, until he was struggling to keep his footing in the slippery place which is not dry land, nor yet over water. Gwydion pushed Pryderi into one of the in-between places, a threshold between this world and the Otherworld. There, where the veil between the worlds was thin, Pryderi suddenly saw his opponent in both worlds: in the guise he had adopted, that of a warrior, and in his true shape as a sorcerer, surrounded by the aura of his power.

In that moment Pryderi acknowledged to himself that he was lost, though he did not cease to strive. He knew then that it would only be a matter of time before Gwydion prevailed and he was slain. From somewhere beyond the bounds of space and time, he heard the song of the Birds of Rhiannon. Their song was for him.

As a hero Pryderi had lived, learning the skills of kingship and those of a warrior. Many times during his story he was pitched against magic, and overcame the trials it put in his way. But, at the last, it was magic which overcame him.

As a hero he died, losing his own life rather than risk the lives with which he was entrusted. The doorway of death opened for him and he stepped beyond time. Like his mother before him, Pryderi moved between worlds; but while her journey brought her from the Otherworld into this world, his took him, at the last, out of the world of his story.

Pryderi fell, his lifeblood bright on Gwydion's blade, though in truth it was Gwydion's magic that had conquered him.

A great groan went up from his war band, to see their leader fall and rise no more. Math, as was fitting in a king, gave orders that Pryderi's body was to be treated with respect, and returned to his people.

In sadness and ceremony, the men of Dyfed buried Pryderi at the meeting place of the two rivers, and marked his grave with a great shaped stone, more than half the height of a man. That stone still stands, set now in the graveyard of a small church in the village of Maentwrog, in the shade of a mighty yew more than one thousand years old.

Then Pryderi's war band left the North lands and went home to Dyfed, carrying the news of the loss of their lord to those who had waited for his return: those who had to mourn for him, grieve for him, and then learn to carry on living without him.

Although their stories continued, Pryderi's story ends here: in the threshold land between two rivers, at a smoothly shaped stone. That stone marks an overlap between the world of the story and the world where the story is remembered, like a reflection of sky and clouds in the water of a river pool.

# Some recommended versions of The Four Branches of the Mabinogion

## In English

John K. Bolland (translator), Anthony
    Griffiths (photographer), *The Mabinogion:
    Legend and Landscape of Wales*, 2006,
    Gwasg Gomer
Sioned Davies (translator), *The Mabinogion*,
    2007, Oxford University Press
Jeffrey Gantz (translator), *The Mabinogion*,

1976, Penguin Classics

Charlotte Guest (translator), *The Mabinogion*,
   1997 edition, Dover Publications version of
   1906 edition

## In Welsh

Alun Ifans, (addasydd), *Pedair Cainc y
   Mabinogi i Ddysgwyr*, 2003, Y Lolfa

Dafydd a Rhiannon Ifans (golygyddion),
   *Y Mabinogion*, 2001, Gwasg Gomer

Gwyn Thomas (addasydd), Margaret Jones
   (arlunydd), *Y Mabinogi*, 1984, Gwasg
   Prifysgol Cymru

## Modern versions

### For adults:

Katy Cawkwell, *The Story of Rhiannon*, 2007,
   Parthian

**FOR CHILDREN:**

**IN WELSH**
Mererid Hopwood, *Straeon o'r Mabinogi*,
   2012, Gwasg Gomer

**IN ENGLISH**
Daniel Morden, *Tree of Leaf and Flame*, 2012,
   Pont Books

If you enjoyed this book, you may also be interested in…

## Denbighshire Folk Tales

FIONA COLLINS

Fiona Collins has collected a wide range of tales here. People unfamiliar with the culture and customs of the county will find some fascinating and unusual tales. Denbighshire has inspired stories of magic, dragons and devils and ordinary people doing extraordinary things.

978 0 7524 5187 9

## Ancient Legends Retold: The Legend of Vortigern

SIMON HEYWOOD

Generations before Arthur's birth, a British warlord looks back on his life. Vortigern's voice speaks from the heart of a forgotten darkness, telling a story of courage and cowardice, glory and crime, tragedy and treason.

978 0 7524 9004 5

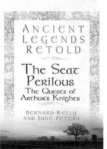

## Ancient Legends Retold: The Seat Perilous

JUNE PETERS AND BERNARD KELLY

The Seat Perilous was the place left for the knight who would one day attain the Grail.. These are the untold tales of the knights who went out into the world and the ladies of the lake they found there.

978 0 7524 8970 4